Cambridge Elements ≡

Elements in Earth System Governance
edited by
Frank Biermann
Utrecht University
Aarti Gupta
Wageningen University

ENVIRONMENTAL HUMAN RIGHTS IN EARTH SYSTEM GOVERNANCE

Democracy beyond Democracy

Walter F. Baber
California State University Long Beach
Robert V. Bartlett
University of Vermont

CAMBRIDGE
UNIVERSITY PRESS

University Printing House, Cambridge CB2 8BS, United Kingdom

One Liberty Plaza, 20th Floor, New York, NY 10006, USA

477 Williamstown Road, Port Melbourne, VIC 3207, Australia

314–321, 3rd Floor, Plot 3, Splendor Forum, Jasola District Centre, New Delhi – 110025, India

79 Anson Road, #06–04/06, Singapore 079906

Cambridge University Press is part of the University of Cambridge.

It furthers the University's mission by disseminating knowledge in the pursuit of education, learning, and research at the highest international levels of excellence.

www.cambridge.org
Information on this title: www.cambridge.org/9781108732352
DOI: 10.1017/9781108762908

First published 2020

A catalogue record for this publication is available from the British Library.

ISBN 978-1-108-73235-2 Paperback
ISSN 2631-7818 (online)
ISSN 2631-780X (print)

Environmental Human Rights in Earth System Governance

Democracy beyond Democracy

Elements in Earth System Governance

DOI: 10.1017/9781108762908
First published online: May 2020

Walter F. Baber
California State University Long Beach

Robert V. Bartlett
University of Vermont

Author for correspondence: Robert V. Bartlett, robert.v.bartlett@uvm.edu

Abstract: Environmental rights are a category of human rights necessarily central to both democracy and effective earth system governance (any environmental/ecological/sustainable democracy). For any democracy to remain democratic, some aspects must be beyond democracy and must not be allowed to be subjected to any ordinary democratic collective choice processes shy of consensus. Real, established rights constitute a necessary boundary of legitimate everyday democratic practice. Baber and Bartlett analyze how human rights are made democratically and, in particular, how they can be made with respect to matters environmental, especially matters that have import beyond the confines of the modern nation-state.

Keywords: democracy; environmental rights; human rights; consensus; environmental governance

ISBNs: 9781108732352 (PB), 9781108762908 (OC)
ISSNs: 2631-7818 (online), 2631-780X (print)

Contents

1 Introduction

Both democratic theorists and democratic activists tend to think of democracy in terms of both who chooses and the processes that determine and structure how choices are made. They avoid confronting a paradox at the heart of democracy: For any democracy to remain democratic, some aspects of democracy must be beyond democracy. That is, some matters must not be allowed to be subject to ordinary democratic collective choice processes (they must remain beyond any democratic choice processes shy of consensus).

Rights can be conceived of as regions of policy space constituting shorthand consensus understandings of what should be, and is, beyond ordinary democracy. Thus, the notion of rights constitutes one boundary of legitimate everyday democratic discourse. Environmental rights are a category of human rights necessarily central to both democracy and global environmental protection and governance (earth system governance democracy).

Yet, consideration of environmental human rights has had minimal impact on thinking about earth system governance. O'Neill (2016, 170) identifies a new focus on how global environmental institutions can "protect and be guided by broader human values, rights and laws" as one of the four key missing ingredients that institutional reform in earth system governance should address. Gupta (2016, 276) argues that the "survival needs of humans should be guaranteed under human rights law" and that this objective can be subsumed under the Earth System Governance Project's analytical heading of equitable access to subsistence goods. But the literature to date has not grappled with the establishment of rights-claims asserting a universal entitlement to the essential environmental preconditions for effective human agency. Such systems of environmental human rights directly link the policy problems of earth system governance to the capabilities of humans for engaging in democratic self-governance – and, in particular, to two of the research lenses identified in the second Earth System Governance Science Plan, namely, justice and allocation, and democracy and power (Burch et al. 2019).

The necessary body of environmental rights required by earth system governance constitutes an expansive subset of human rights, which as rights must be understood to be categorically different from what are often conceived or imagined by nature writers and moral philosophers as the intrinsic rights of nature, animals, ecosystems, landscape features, or Gaia. Recognized environmental human rights have an essentially relational character; they secure agency for every human – "the necessary conditions of human action" (Gewirth 1983, 3). Moreover, human rights "involve requirements or claims of necessary conduct on the part of other persons or groups," imposing reciprocal 'oughts' addressed to others as 'musts' (5–6). A person, therefore, has human rights when he or she can "make morally justified, stringent, effective demands on other persons" that they not interfere with his or her "having the *necessary* goods of action and that they also help him to attain these goods when they cannot be obtained" by his or her own effort (11, emphasis added). This direct connection with the necessary conditions of action, the basic requirements of human agency, is what lends human rights their universality – as against the "more restricted" objectives with which other categories of rights are connected (210).

Environmental rights, like all human rights, have multiple characteristics and vary across any number of continua. Two accounts of how human rights come to be established are the declaratory (which understands rights as being established by definitive declarations in the form of charters, constitutional provisions, or covenants) and the adjudicatory (which understands rights as established by resolution of disputes by widespread recognition of assertions of universal entitlements). If we shift our focus from human rights per se to human rights narratives, two characteristics emerge that are particularly important: the level of abstraction and the degree of reflexivity (descriptive/cognitive/behavioral). Human rights narratives, and environmental rights as a subset of human rights, can be mapped onto the conceptual spaces defined by a normative-analytical frame that incorporates all of these characteristics.

The potential contribution to emerging democratic approaches to earth system governance of both theoretical treatments of environmental rights and the real-world establishment of substantive and procedural environmental rights can be seen in the formation of international regimes and the tradition of legal restate-ments. Both processes are animated by the same desire to document areas of broad consensus about legitimate and desirable ends of public policy. Such searches for such consensus can be augmented through appropriate social scien-tific strategies and memorialized through legal processes including processes that already exist and are reasonably well understood. But consensus itself matters, as can be seen in its implications from the perspectives of history, sociology, and political science. In significant ways, reimagined versions of these reasonably well-understood processes can serve the cause of extending environmental human rights in democratic earth system governance – of developing human rights that address environmental concerns.

Unless specifically qualified, all references to rights in this Element are to real, established (workable and working) human rights. Real, established human rights "have never been a gift – not from God, nor from Nature, nor from kings, nor even from wise founders" (Epp 1998, 197) – nor, for that matter, from philosophers, or prophets, judges, or parliaments, or conferences, or constitutional conventions. Rather, real rights become established and are maintained only in complex political, sociological, and legal processes. Of course, they always originate in moral arguments, declarations, and judgments, but until they have an existence beyond words and imaginations, they remain merely hypothetical. To be real, rights must be so well-established that they are rarely disputed, and real rights must present socially, politically, and legally accepted bounds on what must, can, and cannot be done in the everyday lives of humans.

Moral arguments underlie all rights, and so moral arguments are also foundational for all environmental human rights. Undoubtedly, discourses about environmental ethics, nonreciprocal responsibility, rights of nature, or ecocentricism will foster values and practices compatible with greater ecological sustainability and will continue to contribute to the emergence and establishment of some types of environmental human rights. As such, those discourses will always be important to understanding the normative basis of certain rights. But claims about intrinsic rights are not a focus of analysis in this Element because real, actionable rights of the environment in general, or of any aspects of nature in particular, will always require humans to establish or abolish rights and for humans to exercise those rights. The rights of anything nonhuman require human representation – 'rights of nature' always means the rights of humans to represent nature and to exercise rights on behalf of nature. It may be highly desirable for humans to try to practice virtue ethics or ecological rationality or, in Leopold's evocative phrase, to 'think like a mountain', but ultimately they will be unable to think like anything but human beings. The Arendtian 'right to have rights' is just another way to characterize human agency. It is the ability of humans to arrive at a final vocabulary about the most important relations among them (and them only). It is impossible for nonhumans to participate in that choice – and a choice is precisely what it always is. At the same time, human beings can never transcend their humanness, making true ecocentrism on the part of humans impossible. Even if it were possible, true ecocentrism would demand a degree of misanthropism that no democrat of any variety would ever find acceptable. (The most serious advocates of deep ecology have clarified what true ecocentrism would require, and it would bode poorly for eight or more billion human beings.)

How do real, established human rights come to exist and serve as crucial pillars of functioning democratic systems and, in particular, how *do* they – and how *can* they – become meaningful with respect to matters environmental, matters of earth system governance, especially for matters that have import beyond the confines of the modern nation-state? This is the question at the center of this Element.

2 A Human Rights Foundation for Democratic Earth System Governance?

Aspects of what constitutes 'democracy' continue to be highly contested, but the term can generally be understood to denote a system of governing activity that involves an equal and near-universal right to participate in choosing leaders or policies or otherwise making collective decisions, active participation on the basis of equal citizenship in politics and civic life, equal protection of the human rights of all people, and the rule of law in which behavioral standards and requirements apply equally to all citizens. 'Earth system governance democracy', in turn, denotes a (still only imaginary) system of governing activity that will meet all of these criteria along with the additional demanding expectation that it must functionally, substantively, or procedurally live up to some minimal standard of ecological rationality (Bartlett 1986, Dryzek 1987, Baber and Bartlett 2005). In both popular and theoretical understandings of democracy generally, there is an emphasis and focus, as well as a substantial theoretical and empirical literature, on voting and participation but considerably less attention to rights and the rule of law. Yet, the recognition of a body of human rights that is insulated from popular abridgment by the effective rule of law is absolutely necessary to the continued functioning of any genuine democracy and, therefore by logical extension, to any prospective conception (or any eventual performance) of earth system governance democracy. Development of both robust theories and sustainable practical experiments demands that theorists and reformers (and constructive revolutionaries) attend to the rights and rule of law foundation that democratic earth system governance must have.

It is frequently useful to distinguish substantive rights from procedural rights, and occasionally we do here, yet many procedural rights are really only elaborations, or manifestations, of substantive rights. Few if any other rights distinctions (negative/positive, primary/secondary, distributional rights/rights of distribution, etc.) are conceptually unambiguous, mutually exclusive, or collectively exhaustive either, and all tend to break down in use.

Building upon this general perspective, environmental rights can be conceived of as regions in policy spaces – opportunities, channels, and interactions with potential for policy transformation (McGee 2004, 16) – where the well-known democratic deficit in governance has not resulted in elite processes going 'off track' – spaces where political leaders and those they serve have not parted normative company on the subject of the environment. As a result of the existence of at least some congruence of elite and mass attitudes (Baber and Bartlett 2015), it is increasingly plausible to adopt the term 'rights' as a shorthand label for these areas of policy consensus about claims asserting a universal entitlement. An emerging trialogue between democratic theory, human rights, and environmental protection has yet to transform either humanity or nature in any obvious way – perhaps because it consists largely of three relatively independent dialogues. But the development of a normative consensus on some basic environmental rights has progressed to the point that the case for environmental procedural rights is all but unanswerable and the moral argument for substantive environmental rights as essential preconditions for democratic decision-making is increasingly unimpeachable (Hayward 2000, 2016). After all, some level of consensus is necessary for the development of any 'demos' whatsoever (Risse 2014). As Eckersley (2004, 137) points out, the putative tension between environmentalism and democracy can readily be dispensed with in light of the fact that environmental rights (both procedural and substantive) are "designed to enhance rather than foreclose democratic debate." The point is to "create an environmental due process that minimizes judicial involvement and broadens democratic participation." This developing cluster of rights functions to "improve the conditions and inclusiveness" of the environmental debate by "redressing major power imbalances in political communication and representation."

The dialogic emphasis brought to bear on environmental rights by Eckersley is particularly useful. It allows us to observe that, in this sense, environmental rights function as a sort of "final vocabulary" (Rorty 1989). These rights give us both a terminology that we no longer feel the need to define or defend and a collection of discourses in which that language allows us (sensibly and plausibly) to engage – in this case, on environmental topics (Hajer 1995, Fischer 2003). So, discussed in the literature on environmental liberalism (but not so much yet in the deliberative democratic literature) is the notion of rights as constituting the bounds of legitimate democratic discourse. Meyer (2015), for example, suggests that, although liberalism generally prioritizes the right over the good, it has not been necessary for liberalism to be neutral with respect to different goods or differing conceptions of the good. This partially explains a turn toward liberal environmentalism in the last couple of decades – a turn that Meyer argues has involved efforts to identify how a particular good such as environmental sustainability is consistent with, and likely to be fostered by, liberalism. It also suggests a pathway between environmental liberalism and the green republicanism that some of liberalism's critics think offers the best chance "to achieve the triple bottom line of sustainable development and deal with the connected problems of economic and political inequality and ecological unsustainability" (Barry 2008, 10). Along that pathway, concepts of justice originally held by individuals become institutionalized as societal rules, some of which eventually become global norms – with the most influential ultimately finding their way into international law (Risse, Ropp, and Sikkink 1999, Sikkink 2017).

This potential for liberalism to reconcile itself to both environmental and political critics through a more robust regime of environmental rights may be the primary reason that the right to a healthy environment has gone from an idea merely articulated by Rachel Carson to a concept that is legally recognized (in either constitutional or statutory form) by most nations in the world. This development is not only a "hopeful sign for the future" (Boyd 2012, 290); it also establishes a clear and compelling agenda for the completion of the unfinished foundation of global environmental governance (Boyd 2015). On the one the hand, the "good" of a healthy environment has "found its footing" as a human right because it is a necessary precondition to other "fundamental and widely recognized rights." On the other hand, human rights are increasingly understood to be "important tools of environmental protection" in a world where poverty and dispossession force ecologically unsustainable lives on much of the world's population in pursuit of the goods needed for survival (Conca 2015, 146).

What does it mean to conceptualize the environment as a (at least small) bundle of rights, rather than as a good? Doing so obviously moves environmental sustainability (or at least some aspects of environmental sustainability) beyond the category of a good. If one conceives of rights as the basic tools through which a society pursues justice, democracy would seem to be their constant companion in as much as no 'undemocratic' agent of justice could ever be worthy of the name (Dryzek 2016).

So, it would appear that if human rights are to answer the call to environmental protection, that answer will be couched (at least initially) in the familiar language of political liberalism. The irony here is hard to miss. If it is the concepts and terminology of free enterprise and the Washington Consensus that we hope to use to reverse the ecological damage of breakneck industrialization and to avoid the worst environmental outcomes of globalization, perhaps we have given up the game (and many potential spectators) before play has even begun. Yet, the modern discourse over human rights has as one of its central narratives the battle between liberalism (often identified more closely with neoliberalism than is warranted) and those who believe that modern liberalism imposes a culturally and socially specific conception of rights. By privileging individual rights over collective and cultural rights (for example), it is said that current international regimes allow multinational corporations to overlook both the human and ecological consequences of their endless pursuit of wealth and power (Westra 2011).

A longer historical view paints a different picture. Although charges of cultural bias have long been made against the campaign for human rights, particularly as it was instantiated in the Universal Declaration of Human Rights adopted by the United Nations (UN) in 1948, neither that document nor the movement it advanced are creatures of Western hegemony. Each traces its origins to protagonists from the Global South, activists who were "not motivated by a single liberal philosophy." Moreover, these activists "came from different religious and political traditions. Some were secular, many were not" (Sikkink 2017, 92). One way of thinking about their framing of human rights is that it has been a search for the overlapping consensus between comprehensive world views that Rawls assures us does not need to be politically "indifferent or skeptical" (1993, 150). Even this formulation is not beyond criticism, of course. It is not unreasonable to assume that, under some circumstances, the search for culturally nonspecific consensus (even one based in an interest so clearly shared as environmental protection) will result in a politics so thin that it fails to elicit the level of engagement enjoyed by the thick moralities for which it is a political substitute (Gregg 2003). To the extent that this is true, there is nothing to be said about human rights that can be genuinely global – much less recognizably universal.

But before surrendering to the quietism that this account of the situation might seem to counsel, it may be worthwhile to consider a different conception of human rights – one that has philosophical grounding in Western thought, but is inherently open to redeployment beyond its historical confines. In an observation that was as much anthropological as philosophical, Rorty argues that all human beings "carry about a set of words they employ to justify their actions, beliefs, and their lives." Using these words, we "praise our friends" and show "contempt for our enemies." These are also the terms that we use to explain (to ourselves and to others) our "long-term plans, our deepest self-doubts and our highest hopes." In sum, we use these words to tell, "sometimes prospectively, sometimes retrospectively," the stories of our lives. These words are each person's "final vocabulary" (Rorty 1989, 73).

For Rorty, a vocabulary is final if casting that vocabulary into doubt leaves its user with "no noncircular argumentative recourse" (Rorty 1989, 73). In other words, vocabulary is final for individuals when they reach the limit of their willingness to explain or justify their assertions. Rendered into a form that fits more usefully into a democratic superstructure, a vocabulary is final for a population if it is agreed (as part of a broader political consensus) to refrain from pressing the justificatory regress beyond (or behind) that terminology. Rights, in this sense, are a form of final vocabulary. They can be either a label for a concrete outcome in a specific circumstance that almost no one is willing to criticize *or* the formulation of a normative principle that carries such positive appeal and is stated at such a level of generality that almost no one is willing to dissent from it. The task of the human rights activist or scholar is, then, to proceed inductively (in the first case) or deductively (in the second) to arrive at an interpretation of what a 'right' means to the pragmatic issue at hand. This way of understanding 'human rights work' does not privilege the individual over the collective, the financial over the spiritual, or the Western over the non-Western. It requires only: (1) a willingness to generalize from morally thick judgments about concrete disputes in the direction of thinner covering rules for resolving classes of disputes, and (2) a commitment to search for interpretations of thin but consensual decision rules that move toward an understanding of those rules that can accommodate morally thicker decisions about a broader range of real-world outcomes.

Human environmental rights, so conceived, challenge local knowledge and commitment to seek broader understanding on conceptually higher ground and require cosmopolitan and humanistic insight to strive for wider acceptance within the lived experience of human communities of fate.

Emergent Environmental Rights Consensuses

The potential for this understanding of human rights can be tested by exploring some of the areas in which a level of deliberative consensus sufficient to support environmental rights discourses is being developed, and evidence of that emergent consensus can be found. Policy spaces in which persuasive environmental rights discourses are most likely to emerge from the existing or foreseeable congruence of elite and popular environmental norms include: (1) involving access to information and decision-making processes; (2) ensuring access to food and water; and (3) providing environmental security to all. Even a brief superficial analysis of current and necessary future trajectories of these environmental rights discourses suggests how regions of emerging consensus extend the reach of environmental protection norms without either diluting a consensus into meaninglessness or depriving democratic politics of its critical capacity. The ultimate task, of course, will be to suggest how those discourses might be reconciled with the socially and culturally diverse legal traditions in which environmental rights would have to be acquitted.

Access to Environmental Information and Decision-Making

Success in the areas of environmental and human rights litigation (as in any other) begins with an understanding of legal procedure and how to use it. In a plural society there may be more widespread support for procedural rights than substantive ones when it comes to potentially divisive issues. Moreover, a sound procedural footing is useful insurance against falling into the absolutist view of environmental rights in a futile attempt to "take them out of the hurly-burly of politics and give them a higher status" than judges are ever likely to confer upon them (Bodansky 2010, 61).

A second and more specific reason for beginning with the procedural rights of information and access to decision-making is that our objective is to find productive ways of relating the emerging field of international environmental rights to the principles and practices of democracy, in particular deliberative democracy. The relationship between deliberative democracy and environmental protection more generally has been explored at both the national and global levels (Baber and Bartlett 2005, 2009). A prominent feature of this relationship has been a tension between two values that deliberative democrats hold dear – a commitment to rational discourse in search for consensus and a dedication to diversity and inclusion. This tension is persistent, and the fact that it can be resolved (Baber and Bartlett 2015, 57–82) does not mean that it will eventually go away on its own. Affirmative and authoritative actions to satisfy people's needs for information (in support of discursive rationality) and access (of a universal character) will obviously be part of any strategy for developing politically sustainable resolutions of that recurring tension that might ultimately safeguard environmental rights.

Information and access as an area of inquiry has an additional advantage – the availability of a fully developed and formally adopted international agreement on the subject. The Convention on Access to Information, Public Participation in Decision-making and Access to Justice in Environmental Matters (Aarhus Convention) was signed in 1998 in the Danish city of Aarhus and entered into force in 2001. Currently, it has forty-seven parties – forty-six states and the European Union on behalf of all of its twenty-eight member states. The Aarhus Convention recognizes public rights regarding access to information, public participation, and access to justice in governmental decision-making processes on matters concerning the local, national, and transboundary environment. It focuses on interactions between the citizens and public authorities.

More specifically, the convention requires that every citizen should have the right to wide and easy access to environmental information, that public authorities must collect and disseminate information in a timely and transparent manner, that the public must be informed regarding all environmentally relevant projects and must have the chance to participate during decision-making and legislative processes, and that the public has the right to judicial or administrative recourse procedures in case of violations of existing environmental law or the principles of the convention itself (Duyck 2015). Although compliance with the convention by government actors is not uncontested, as one might imagine, finding evidence of serious dissent from the convention's purposes and provisions in mass public opinion is nearly impossible. But that does not mean that the convention's underlying policy theory enjoys the level of support – either by states or a global public – that its full effectiveness requires.

As with other 'transparency' policies (Gupta and Mason 2014), the Aarhus Convention assumes that with adequate information, access to decision-making, and effective legal recourse, an enlightened public can exercise the control over its elected and appointed officials that democracy and protection of the environment require. Few would argue with the objective, but there is considerable evidence that each connection of that predictive discourse is subject to being undermined by public attitudes. For instance, receiving full information regarding public issues (particularly where the information is persistently negative) has the potential to discourage public participation in the policy process (Bauhr and Grimes 2015).

Citizens are often willing to defer to public officials rather than hold them accountable. This pattern persists even in the presence of policy outcomes that are regarded as significantly negative and can be traced to the popular assumption that government officials are possessed of a level of expertise that justifies an attitude of deference rather than strict accountability (Gerber et al. 2011). It is even possible to convince majorities in developed democracies (as a result of campaigns promoting judicial retrenchment in defense of existing power and privilege) that free and equal access to the halls of justice is a policy problem rather than a solution (Staszak 2015). So, in spite of its attractiveness in principle, Aarhus harbors within its normative foundation a number of potentially serious lacunae. The existing level of consensus that supports the convention leaves it vulnerable in nation-states whose elites are reluctant to bring their domestic procedures into alignment with the principles that Aarhus espouses (Getliffe 2002).

Eat, Drink, and Be Human: Rights to Food and Water

As a general matter, thinking about rights tends to run strongly in the direction of procedures. But when substantive rights are asserted, they tend to fall into the categories of political rights and property rights – with social and economic rights receiving less recognition, if they are granted any position at all. This relatively simple and widely recognized fact goes some way toward explaining the confusing state in which the right to food and water is found. There is a patchwork quilt of global, regional, and national documents related in more or less direct and explicit ways to these two fundamental human needs – often without invoking the concept of rights at all. Yet, together these two emerging human rights discourses have significant potential as grounds for legal advocacy in the cause of environmental protection.

Access to food as a matter of being a fundamental human right is the product of a cluster of international and regional norm-building efforts. The normative core of this process is not that people should be given food but, rather, that people are entitled to enjoy the preconditions, including environmental, necessary to feed themselves (Kent 2005). This is the central organizing principle that defines the contours of a justiciable claim on national governments that has both negative and positive dimensions, and that has found its way into both international and regional legal documents such as the 1948 Universal Declaration of Human Rights and the 1966 International Covenant on Economic, Social and Cultural Rights (ICESCR). The right became justiciable under the terms of the 2009 Optional Protocol to the ICESCR and the 2012 Food Assistance Convention. The principle is enshrined in more specific international agreements on genocide and the status of refugees and in conventions regarding the rights of women, children, and the disabled – as well as in numerous regional agreements and national constitutional and statutory schemes. At its most ambitious, the principle calls for nothing less than a devolution of food sovereignty that would allow people (and peoples) to reclaim control over this most basic relationship between themselves and their environment (Claeys 2015). Careful case analyses of how this principle is sustained by practice identify a broad range of legal, political, and economic circumstances that produce widely varying results in developed (Wernaart 2014) and developing (Riol 2016) countries alike.

Likewise, the human right to water is a legal discourse with a long and varied pedigree (Salmon and McInerney-Lankford 2004). The main international agreements that explicitly recognize a right to water (and the collateral right to sanitation) are the 1979 Convention on the Elimination of All Forms of Discrimination against Women, the 1989 Convention on the Rights of the Child, and the 2008 Convention on the Right of Persons with Disabilities. The right to water would seem to be an essential condition imposed by any of the documents mentioned earlier regarding the right to secure one's own food. As with the right to food, the discourse concerning the right to water relies upon states to attend to any obligations that the right might impose, which necessarily must include protecting the environment. As one might expect, that process relies as much (if not more) on national constitutional and statutory schemes of water rights as it does on international agreements.

As is obvious from even this brief account, the right to water exists under international law but in a more differentiated and multilevel manner than is commonly recognized. The right is neither singular nor comprehensive, neither truly international nor entirely local. It should be understood as a composite discourse carried on at different levels of governance and in different policy arenas. It derives from separate rights to health, life, and an adequate standard of living, and is supported by an array of regional and national rights. As a consequence of its multilevel and multisectoral character, the right to water can only be acquitted in practice by a multipronged legal approach. That approach will necessarily involve (at a minimum) independent international monitoring, national-level enforcement directed at the private sector, and further progressive realization at the international level (Thielborger 2014). The same is true of the right to food discourse. At the international level, both discourses rely largely on ostensibly nonenvironmental agreements (e.g., the UN ICESCR and the Convention of the Rights of the Child) and both pose significant challenges for advocates of international environmental protection.

With respect to the ecological issues associated with efforts to secure the right to food, such efforts may come into conflict with other concerns for environmental protection. The environmental consequences of the Green Revolution are a case in point. Ecological damage was sometimes the direct result of new hybridization, fertilizer, and pest control technologies. But also policies often promoted injudicious use of agricultural inputs and the expansion of production into marginal areas that could not support high levels of agricultural exploitation (Perry 2016). A human rights approach can set up conflicts, pitting food provision, environmental protection, and other human interests against each other in local and international versions of the same divisive and damaging arguments that play out in national political arenas.

Even when environmental rights discourses do not lead to conflicts between environmental protection and other human interests, they have the potential to distract us from the underlying problems that should concern us most. Technophobia is one manifestation of this kind of distraction. Another is the tendency of rights discourses to raise distributional issues. The multiplicity of discourses involved in the human right to water is a prime example. The dominant discourse in this area involves the wide-ranging implications of such a right for the distribution of water. Examining these implications requires putting the right to water into the broader context of different water uses, and also requires analyzing its linkages to (and competition with) other human rights – many of which depend on water for their realization. This focus is a natural consequence of the fact that water allocation is a highly political issue reflecting societal power relations, with existing distribution patterns often benefiting the privileged and powerful. But human rights, broadly speaking, require prioritizing the most basic needs of all people. The right to water obviously has the potential to address these underlying structural causes of the lack of access. Rooted in inequalities and poverty, people can be empowered to hold the state accountable to live up to its human rights obligations and to demand that their basic needs are met (Winkler 2012). A justifiable focus on distributive injustice in water allocation also runs the risk of delaying pursuit of (or even distracting us from) the equally important issues of environmental injustice in the distribution of water pollution impacts and the water needs for ecosystem maintenance, as well as the even broader issue of the water rights problems associated with climate change. Similarly, although a right to *clean* water could have a positive impact on environmental pollution problems, and a right to water could help to protect people in the face of climate-induced drought, it also has the potential to be harmful by prioritizing immediate human needs for water use over longer-term ecosystem maintenance and preservation needs.

Environmental Security in an Insecure Age

The assertion of the general entitlement to a healthy environment as a right *in itself* – to environmental security, as it were – "does not enjoy widespread recognition in international law," in spite of the fact that it "sits at the intersection of a two-way instrumentality" (Conca 2015, 146). On occasion, international human rights law has addressed the right to a healthy environment directly (UNEP 2014). Yet, the plodding international progress toward a right of environmental security has not prevented at least ninety-two nations from incorporating an explicit general environmental right into their constitutions or the high courts of twelve other nations from ruling that such a right is implicit in other provisions of their fundamental law (Boyd 2012, 279).

Before celebrating the intrepidity of national governments for having stepped in where international actors fear to tread, it is worth observing that the actual application of these environmental security provisions continues to be a hit-and-miss affair. As with environmental protection generally, compliance with these rights-based rules has been complicated by the presence of actors who could meet their legal obligations if they wished, but do not, and those who wish to meet their obligations, but cannot. More interesting for our purposes, there is an important similarity across the cases where national courts have taken firm action to enforce a general right of environmental security.

Two standout cases have arisen in the Philippines and in India – involving actions to force water-quality improvements in Manila Bay and to clean up motor vehicle pollution in Delhi. In both instances, the country's high court took definitive action – based at least in part on general environmental security provisions of the sort we have been discussing (Boyd 2012, 168–169, 175–182). In each case, the court was asked to apply a general and open-ended right in a specific and limited way. Both cases presented claims involving spatial and sectoral limits. Neither asked the court to mandate nationwide remedies to secure for the population vital environmental goods or services or impose omnibus regulations to protect the country at large from environmental harm. This suggests that even where broadly worded substantive environmental rights are adopted, at least early on they are likely to be applied by courts in limited doses to address specific ailments. Whether such limited therapy can address the underlying causes of environmental rights violations, much less stem the global pandemic of environmental degradation, is far from clear, as is the prospect of courts engaging in broader, more robust applications.

Nevertheless, in more than half the countries of the world, the explicit right to a healthy environment exists today as a legal rule of general application (Boyd 2012, Gellers 2017). It is true that, where it exists, that right is subject to the same trade-off against other rights that plagues human rights laws generally. Yet it is important to note that the woebegone nation-state has shown itself widely able to entrench a general environmental human right that the international community discusses largely as an abstract and academic possibility. Much of the search for the normative rules that might sustain environmental human rights must still be undertaken at the national level. This is unavoidable if what is sought is more than the expression of aspirational abstractions – the establishment of meaningful entitlements.

Environmental Rights as a Subject Within, and a Constituent Element of, the Human Rights Context

The Universal Declaration of Human Rights, adopted by the UN General Assembly in 1948, has been characterized as a declaration of interdependence. In this view, the declaration, when read as a whole as it was meant to be, is "an integrated document that rests on a concept of the dignity of the human person within the human family" – that it is, in substance as well as form, a declaration of the "interdependence of people, nations, and rights" (Glendon 2002, 174). This is consistent with the argument of those most closely associated with its creation that the declaration's separation of human rights into four categories – rights to life, liberty, and personal security (Articles 3–11), rights in civil society (Articles 12–17), rights in the polity (Articles 18–21), and economic, social, and cultural rights (Articles 22–27) – is not in any way an ordinal, priority, or hierarchical arrangement. The declaration does not view one category of rights as more fundamental, as more necessarily human. Nor does it allow for other distinctions between human rights (procedural v. substantive, negative v. positive, primary v. secondary) to carry much analytical weight – or, indeed, to survive much past the limits of the pedagogical utility. To pursue such distinctions very far is (from the perspective of the declaration) to court one Procrustean dilemma after another.

Therefore, introducing environmental rights into the context of the declaration should not, cannot, be viewed as simply adding another action item to the category of economic, social, and cultural rights. The declaration itself doesn't partition the human experience into such neat packages and, if that kind of view were ever environmentally warranted, it certainly no longer is. Humans are no longer mere survivalists struggling to adapt to their natural environment (although many are still doing that, in part). As a species, our impact on the earth has caused changes that are far outside the range of natural variability, equivalent to such major geological disruptions as ice ages. Scientists are increasingly of the opinion that we are in an entirely new epoch in planetary history: the Anthropocene. In this era of planet-wide anthropogenic transformation, no element of the nonhuman world is immune to human influence and no human interest can be pursued in isolation from ecological considerations (Biermann 2014). It is difficult to escape the conclusion that we need a new model for planet-wide environmental politics, ultimately a "hyper-reflexive geopolitan democracy" for earth system governance (Eckersley 2017). But if this is going to be a truly democratic politics, every structure exercising governance powers needs to have a complementary system of rights – preferably, coextensive with the system of powers that it modifies and guides. The creation of power to govern human environmental impacts demands establishment of environmental human rights sufficient to regulate that new governance capacity, thus securing for it democratic legitimacy.

The ubiquity of concern for environmental rights in governance processes generally is suggested by the pronounced trend toward the inclusion of environmental rights in the constitutions (or basic laws) of nations around the world (Boyd 2012, Gellers 2017). The total number of nations with at least one such provision now numbers over 130, and at least one nation every year since 1971 has added an environmental provision or strengthened one that it already had (Boyd 2015). But even our early experience with these new provisions counsels caution. It is becoming increasingly clear that substantive environmental rights without complementary procedural components usually fail to protect human interests (often due to a lack of justiciability) and that procedural environmental rights (by themselves) guarantee nothing more than that ecologically disastrous decisions will be made after due process. The early difficulties encountered in translating these environmental rights into the language of international law, even in a world where the vast majority of national languages already contain the necessary vocabulary, shows that scalability is a more daunting problem than mutual incomprehension (Morrow 2015).

Perhaps no better example of a fundamental, and environmentally dependent, human right can be imagined than the right to food of adequate quantity and quality, discussed earlier. This topic will clearly appear near the top of most people's list of economic concerns. Yet the number of people worldwide who suffer from food insecurity is approximately one billion, and every five seconds a child dies from hunger (Leib 2011). No wonder, then, that the right to food was explicitly mentioned in the Universal Declaration (Article 25) and in many subsequent international documents. The common understanding of this right is that it embraces "accessibility to food, its quality, its sustainability, and its cultural suitability" (Leib 2011, 147). But the right to food is far from being a simple economic right. Myriad connections tie this concern back to the rights of humans in their polity (disenfranchisement in food governance), in civil society (respecting cultural food preferences and prohibitions), and the life, liberty, and security concerns that contribute so significantly to human dignity (as when starvation becomes a tool of systematic repression, or even genocide). Food insecurity is clearly implicated in a range of other environmental and human rights concerns. For instance, food insecurity is an important nexus between the problems of global climate change, one the one hand, and forced migration and ongoing refugee crises, on the other (McAdam 2012).

So, if we take the Universal Declaration of Human Rights as our touchstone and fundamental guide to what our species should aspire to (as its authors hoped), perhaps we will need to make more explicit its declaration of inter-dependence (such as can be found, for example, in the 2015 Sustainable Development Goals). We cannot preoccupy ourselves with the procedural versus the substantive, the negative versus the positive, the local versus the global, or the human versus the environmental. Not only are people, nations, and rights mutually independent, all three stand in a relation of interdependence with the nonhuman environment. Neither our fate as a species nor our dignity as persons can be disentangled from the impact we have on the only ecological niche we have ever had – or are likely ever to have in the foreseeable future.

Real-world earth system governance democracy without an effective system of environmental rights, in any circumstances remotely similar to modernity, is impossible. As is often the case when environmental governance developments over recent decades are assessed, reasons can be found to be hopeful (although certainly not enough to justify optimism). An international and increasingly global consensus about certain fundamental environmental rights has emerged in recent decades as a continuation of a broader rights revolution. Although development has been greater in some areas than others, and such rights are still largely observed in the breach, much more has been established than is gen-erally appreciated, and it likewise has been more consequential. We can expect that efforts will continue to be made to extend the environmental reach of that revolution, although we can be confident that its path and speed will never be smooth, with neither its direction nor impacts ever especially predictable. Reversals, as is true of human rights generally, are undoubtedly possible. But if something approximating ecological democracy is ever to be realized in the human environment – something beyond the imaginings of theorists and utopian fiction writers – then it will be necessary for a significant body of environmental rights to be universally recognized, and for governance arrangements to be created that will give them substantive impact via an extended rule of law. In the Anthropocene, life itself (in all its forms) is threatened by perversely managerial forms of democracy (Wolin 2004) and by increasingly totalitarian politics untempered by the genuinely political (Wolin 2008) – circumstances in which environmental rights become ever more essential, not simply to redress environmental wrongs but also to frame environmental obligations. To successfully contest the Janus-faced process of ecological despoliation and human exploitation, real ecological democracy must rely on established, embedded, robust configurations of environmental rights to clearly identify "those who should not have done what they did, those who should have done what they didn't, and those who must act now because of what others did and didn't do" (Walzer 2007, 262).

3 Mapping Transnational Environmental Rights for Democratic Earth System Governance

Human rights have multiple characteristics and vary across any number of continua. Two models or accounts of human rights are a declaratory model and an adjudicatory model. Shifting focus from human rights per se to human rights narratives, two characteristics emerge that are particularly important: their level of abstraction and their degree of reflexivity (which can range from descriptive to cognitive to behavioral). In order to arrive at a better (more complete) understanding of environmental rights as a subset of human rights, human rights narratives can be mapped onto the conceptual spaces defined by typologies incorporating all of these characteristics. Both existing theoretical treatments of environmental rights and the real-world establishment of substantive and procedural rights have profound implications for the prospects of democratic earth system governance. Further theoretical and empirical research is needed to determine the degree of international support for environmental rights, assess the authenticity of any congruence between elite and popular opinion, and anticipate how environmental rights narratives might be received by humanity's varying legal traditions. That research can only be carried out effectively if it is based on a clear conceptual framework.

Pieces of a Puzzle

> . . . rooted in a substantive view of human nature . . . human rights set the limits and requirements of social (especially state) action, but that action, guided by human rights, plays a major role in realizing that 'nature'. . . . They create the type of person posited in the underlying moral vision. (Donnelly 2013, 15)

There is a persistent puzzle at the heart of the human rights discourse. It is captured, unintentionally we imagine, in the title of Donnelly's (2013) text on the subject, *Universal Human Rights in Theory and Practice*. We refer here not to the clause that distinguishes theory from practice, but rather to its antecedent. Concerning the rights people care about most, are they *universal* or are they *human*? This dichotomy of rights may strike some as peculiar, or even false, but as a dichotomy of rights *discourses*, it is a useful distinction to draw – especially when the ultimate objective is to better understand environmental human rights and the mutual "limits and requirements" between and among the universe and its human elements. Before turning attention to that particular subspecies of human rights, however, a more general discussion of human rights (and the dichotomy we suggest) is in order.

In the popular imagination, the subject of human rights has been dominated by what Donnelly (2013) calls the "universal declaration model." His reference, of course, is to the Universal Declaration of Human Rights, adopted by the UN in 1948. The history of that document is well known. A small group of remarkable men and women, led by the redoubtable Eleanor Roosevelt, worked feverishly to exploit a window of opportunity between the end of World War II and the impending Cold War that already darkened humanity's horizon. Taking advantage of the still fresh horror of the Holocaust before a new but war-weary world became ideologically divided and institutionally ossified, they managed to fashion one of that new world's founding documents – a 'bill of rights' to go with the Charter of the UN (Glendon 2002). As creation myths go, this is a pretty good one. It features a pivotal moment in history, a heroine who thinks only of others while battling her own personal grief, and a cast of supporting players each worthy of books of their own. Unlike many other myths, it has the added benefit of extensive supporting documentation.

To speak of a Universal Declaration model, however, is to take a useful step back from periods, places, and people. Both the contingencies and the inevitabilities of the document fall away, leaving its basic concepts and the intentions of its authors more readily visible. When we take this backward step, we begin to see human rights less as a declaration and more as a declaratory process – a collection of ever-developing narratives. How we understand that the source and subject of these narratives then becomes an open question. It is fine to say that human rights are universal, but what part of the universe serves as their author?

One attribution of 'authorship' is the claim that there are certain characteristics common to all human beings, a feature of the human universe, that mandate a particular list of rights. From the American Declaration of Independence to the French Declaration of the Rights of Man and Citizen, back to the US Bill of Rights, and on to the Universal Declaration, history offers many examples of what on this account are merely translations and elaborations of the same story (Arendt 1994 [1948]). Rights are universal because human nature makes certain nonnegotiable demands that vary little from place to place and across the span of our history. If rights are simply a matter of recognition through declaration, then the central challenge they pose is one of *justification* – largely involving an effort to apply to increasingly specific circumstances the rights we have declared in order to show that they are, indeed, human rights. First, one fleshes out a declaration into a treaty or convention. Either as part of that process, or immediately after it, an *institution* of governance is created and charged with the *implementation* of the terms of the convention. It is through the process of implementation that we finally discover the human significance of our universal declaration. Like the American historians' parlor game of 'name the greatest presidents' (in which choosing the great defines greatness itself), the process of declaration and justification of rights aspires to become a recursive algorithm – in which justifying the smaller part of the larger whole is expected to eventually provide us an understanding of both the whole and of wholeness (humanness) itself. Rights are there, implicit in our very nature, waiting to be discovered. Their history is incidental. We need only summon the courage to declare them and then to justify our declarations – and through their justification, make them universal.

There is, however, an alternative to this 'declaratory' theory of rights. This alternative emphasizes processes of *adjudication* (the resolution of concrete disputes, through adversarial or inquisitorial procedure or some combination of the two, often in front of a neutral arbiter) over the process of declaration. This adjudicatory view regards rights as the spoils of a successful revolution – fought, not by radicals in the streets, but by advocates in neutral fora such as courts, commissions, and tribunals. In the Western context, this revolution realizes it fullest development and shows its greatest strength "through an interaction between supportive judges and the support structure for right-advocacy litigation" (Epp 1998, 197). A previous authoritative declaration of rights is by no means necessary, as has been demonstrated repeatedly around the world with respect to, for example, abortion, same-sex marriage, and crimes against humanity. This alternate creation myth, like the declaratory mythology of the Universal Declaration, poses its own particular challenge. It is all well and good to win a battle, to achieve for a specific individual the legal outcome that he or she is seeking through a process that is unapologetically adversarial. It is another thing altogether (a more collaborative or consensual process) to find resolutions to larger conflicts and from those concrete outcomes and to craft more general propositions that could be set out as rights – as, in short, a rule that one might justly expect to be followed in other similar circumstances. The challenge, then, is to *consolidate* the winnings of particular cases in ways that promote future adjudicatory successes that (eventually) amount to new moral expectations of specific kinds of legal outcomes. Thus, the declaratory and adjudicatory approaches to the development of human rights work in opposite (though not necessarily inconsistent) directions along a continuum from the abstract to the concrete (as suggested in Table 1).

The adjudicatory account of where rights come from is, by its very nature, far more human than it is universal. It emphasizes that rights are the product of human communities and their efforts to solve concrete problems. Moreover, it clearly suggests that "if human rights are derived from communities, and if any given political community is contingent and particular, then human rights are themselves contingent and culturally particular" rather than universal in any fundamental sense (Gregg 2012, 215). This observation puts the challenge of *consolidating* human rights won through adjudicatory processes in a new light. Individual communities, existing as political entities, have a variety of alternatives for consolidating litigation outcomes. In communities with a common law tradition, *restatement* is a plausible alternative – involving the analysis of large numbers of related judgments and the derivation of a covering rule that explains the outcomes in a way that is both complete and parsimonious. In the hands of lawyers and judges, this rule then functions much like a right, giving rise to a morally legitimate expectation that new cases as they occur will be resolved consistent with the restated rule. So long as there are so few adjudicatory processes at the international level (Baber and Bartlett 2009), there can be

Table 1 Two models of human rights

Level/model	Declaratory	Adjudicatory
Most abstract	Declaration ↓	International agreement
Abstract	Convention	Domestic legislation
Concrete	Institutionalization	Restatement
Most concrete	Implementation	↑ 'Litigation'

no equivalent process of restatement, as international agreements are by their very nature declaratory – there is no dispute resolution in them to 'restate'. Nevertheless, restating the decisions of the apex courts of nation-states (in the same way that a common law restatement summarizes decision in subnational jurisdictions) represents a transnational option.

Another more obvious option is to substitute legislation for litigation – that is to say, to adopt a statutory or constitutional framework that institutionalizes legal rights and obligations consistent with a covering rule derived from the same 'database' of particular cases that support restatement. The option to legislate might be regarded as preferable to restatement – both for the sake of clarity and coherence and because it might be regarded as more democratic and (hence) more legitimate. Indeed, the creation of model codes and eventual legislation is one objective of the restatement process as it is conventionally understood. One of legislation's obvious weakness, however, is scalability. If the political community that has identified a right through some form of adversarial process is not coterminous with an appropriate political jurisdiction, for example, because it is either something less than or something more than a state (Gregg 2016), then the ability to legislate may prove elusive. How, then, does one imagine that rights as the adjudicatory products of community life might assert themselves – first, outward from a political community to an entire country, and then onward from the country to the world? Here we eventually reengage with the question of universality. The process of making rights both real and universal can be imagined in at least two distinct (but not necessarily inconsistent) ways. First, *human* rights can become universal by being adopted more or less uniformly by all of the world's nation-states. Second, rights thought to be *universal* can become human by being adopted internationally through conventions that include provisions for implementation or enforcement that are sufficiently strong and adaptable to make those rights real in the lives of human beings regardless of where they reside.

For the first approach to work, much work remains to be done in providing the supportive structure for successful human rights litigation to be pursued worldwide. Generally speaking, this structure consists of "rights-advocacy lawyers, rights-advocacy organizations, and sources of funding" (Epp 1998, 18). Judicial independence, the rule of law, and other institutional characteristics of legal systems are not unrelated to the success of rights litigation, but they are not the central and immediate determinants of the success of broad-based rights revolutions. Where these revolutions have succeeded, "a support structure for civil rights and liberties litigation propelled rights issues" into higher political salience, "encouraged the courts to render favorable decisions and, at least to some extent, provided the judiciary with active partners in the fight against opponents of implementation of these new rights" (22). The gains in legal doctrine achieved through litigation then underwent consolidation, in the form of new administrative rules, training for government employees in compliance with these rules, and systems of internal compliance oversight. Ultimately, law-inspired administrative reform "remade the professional norms and identities of the managerial professions, shifting them decisively from a celebration of insulated discretionary expertise to a celebration of fidelity to legal norms" (Epp 2009, 216). Cross-national studies of the emergence of strong human rights regimes have demonstrated the recurring relevance of this process of litigation and consolidation (Boyd 2012). But even to describe the phenomena where it has occurred is to call to mind the myriad of obstacles to replicating the process worldwide.

The second (and often subsequent) approach – devising strong, substantive, and specific human rights conventions that can command the assent of virtually all nations – would seem to present an even greater challenge than encouraging broader scope and greater uniformity among national human rights regimes. Virtually every nation on earth solemnly rehearses its commitment to human rights on a regular basis – with the worst rights offenders often holding forth the loudest and longest. The language of human rights has become the lingua franca of global moral discourse, and yet there is little evidence of a marked decrease in human rights violations. One might conclude, not unreasonably, that human rights discourses do not translate well into a universal language capable of making itself clearly understood. In the alternate, one could argue that global human rights discourses serve their *genuine* purpose quite well. A cynical view (known immodestly as 'realism' among its subscribers) holds that human rights discourses are designed to do exactly what they have done – conceal the fundamental disagreement among nations about what public morality and the public interest requires while allowing political elites maximum flexibility in the allocation of their resources and the justification of their actions on the world stage. The cynic (or realist) would expect to find a large number of vague agreements, covering a wide range of human concerns, but lacking even the most rudimentary enforcement provisions (Posner 2014). This view predicts precisely the current state of international human rights law.

But is the view of the cynic/realist the only way to assemble the pieces of the puzzle of universal human rights? Is not there a more optimistic, even useful, pattern that one can make of the pieces that realists use to discourage and depress the rest of us? Might there even be, perhaps, a few missing puzzle pieces, the discovery of which would change the overall picture?

Filling in the Puzzle: The Dual Character of Human Rights Narratives

At least one noted human rights scholar has already drawn attention to some unwanted by-products of the way that human rights are often discussed. Glendon (1991) warned that "stark, simple rights dialect of human rights" had put a damper on "the processes of public justification, communication, and deliberation upon which the continuing vitality of a democratic regime depends" (171). To be fair, Glendon was speaking of a domestic rights narrative that in her view had become the "thin edge of a wedge" that was dividing Americans from each other and undermining their ability to reason together about the challenges that they faced. Ironically, these were precisely the rights narratives that Epp (1998) was celebrating (at nearly the same time) as the driving force behind a rights revolution that was finally reining in the excesses of a caveat emptor society that reserved the right to refuse service to anyone. That two human rights scholars, whose objectives are so nearly the same, could have been so divided in their views suggests more than that they were simply looking at two different parts of the same whole. It suggests that the whole may not be fully visible to either, so the parts that attracted their particular attention lacked the interpretive context that was required.

When we shift our attention from human rights to human rights *narratives*, we discover that these narratives can vary along any number of continua. Two of these are particularly important – their level of *abstraction* (which we have already encountered in discussion of the declaratory and adjudicatory models of human rights) and their degree of *reflexivity*. *Abstract* narratives aspire to the greatest scope, to be sensible in the widest variety of circumstances, whereas *concrete* narratives seek the truest representation of rights in specific cases. *Reflexivity* has to do with the purpose(s) that narratives seek to achieve. Is it a *descriptive* narrative that aims only to mark out (to call attention to) subject matter for those to whom it is addressed? Does it aspire to impose some *cognitive* order on the arena of discourse it addresses – to organize its subject matter to allow its addressees to better understand their situation? Or does it actually seek to add to the *behavioral* repertoire – not only to describe and impose cognitive order but to increase the range of potential actions of its addressees for altering their situation? These two dimensions of thought are fundamental characteristics of all narratives that are theoretical or philosophical in nature – whether the narratives are fundamentally normative or analytical. Taken together, they provide a useful framework for comparing those narratives across time and cultures (Collins 1998). A graphic illustration of this normative-analytic typology is in Table 2.

Table 2 A normative-analytic typology of human rights narratives

Level/reflexivity	Descriptive	Cognitive	Behavioral
Most abstract	Aspirational	Inputs	Affective
	Institutional	Throughput	Explanatory
	Programmatic	Outputs	Strategic
Most concrete	Material	Outcomes	Critical

In comparing Table 2 to Table 1, one immediately notices that the horizontal axis no longer describes a nominal set of categories. It is now an ordinal scale that represents, not the narrative method of human rights discourses, but various (increasingly reflexive) purposes that might be served by human narratives. Understanding narratives in this way allows us to disaggregate the universe of possible addressees and to analyze narratives in terms of their potential to achieve their intended (normative) results among their target audiences. This process invites us to distinguish more concretely the various narrative categories from which the concepts of human rights are assembled. For instance, rights narratives that are basically *descriptive* in character can range from the aspirational (e.g., an environment sufficient to sustain human flourishing) to the material (basic nourishment and shelter). Other narratives, which have more *cognitive* (or analytical) objectives, might focus our attention on rights narratives as complex systems for the conversion (throughput) of demands and resources (inputs) into specific policies (outputs) with identifiable consequences (outcomes). Finally, rights narratives with fundamentally *behavioral* (or educative) purposes might have many of the same objectives of other 'educational' traditions or practices – ranging from affective (attitudinal) change and the enhancement of our explanatory capacity to the identification of the behavioral variables most susceptible to purposeful (strategic) manipulation and the critical assessment of real-world behaviors (including criticism itself).

Armed with this normative-analytic typology, one is able to 'map' various rights narratives onto the conceptual space that the typology defines, gaining insight into the relative strengths (or advantages) and weakness (or disadvantages) of those narratives. For example, the narratives of rights advocates like Mary Wollstonecraft (2008 [1790–1794]) who find their inspiration in God's law, tend strongly to cluster in the upper-left cells of Table 2. Their arguments tend to be highly abstract, showing limited interest in either analytical precision or educational-behavioral objectives. They are still characteristic of the declaratory approach to human rights, assuming as they do that a proper (largely intuitive) understanding of the narrative itself is tantamount to successful (affective) conversion of one's interlocutor. At the opposite corner of the discursive territory of human rights, one might expect to find the anti-globalization narratives of those whose rights narratives are unquestionably normative but arise largely from the passion that their critique of immediate circumstances and the strategic-moral imperatives that those circumstances suggest (Stiglitz 2017). Polite as they often are in their manner, the messengers of this perspective are the shock troops of human rights revolutions – 'litigating' human rights in the streets when they feel that they must. It should be no surprise that as these revolutionaries fan out across the normative-analytic map of human rights, their encounters with their declaratory cousins often give rise to a degree of mutual incomprehension – the flavor of which is captured by the juxtaposition of Epp's uplifting enthusiasm and Glendon's sobering contemplation.

It is worth pausing to emphasize that there are no distinctive democratic implications of either model, no democratic advantages of one over the other. Each model is an 'origins' narrative. There is no reason to think that either model is more or less likely to lead to advancement or protection of democratic governance. Neither is more or less subject to being distorted or perverted by elite domination. Those who wish to subvert democracy are always willing to exploit any narrative that suits their purposes. When that happens, only a naive essentialism would think that the fault lies with the narrative.

If this preliminary account of existing human rights narratives has verisimilitude, the next reasonable step is to see how contemporary narratives of environmental rights map onto its normative-analytic framework. The purpose of this exercise is to arrive at a better (more complete) understanding of environmental rights, showing a way forward in advancing our commitment to the reconciliation of environmental sustainability and enhancement of the lived human experience.

Mapping Global Environmental Rights Narratives for Earth System Governance

When the time comes to map the declaratory and adjudicatory models of human rights of Table 1 onto a framework that focuses on narratives (by adding an analytical content to the horizontal axis), an interesting revision of prior assumptions becomes possible. Thought of as narratives, declaratory and adjudicatory human rights no longer seem to run in opposing directions (top-to-bottom and from the ground-up, respectively). Their predominant movement is now in the same direction along the horizontal axis of Table 1. At the highest level of abstraction, the declaratory model boldly announces the *aspiration* to secure new rights by introducing new *inputs* into the global political system (in the form of demands that those rights be protected and support for the steps necessary to achieve them) and relies on the *affective* force of its argument to produce the required behavioral responses. Declaratory rights narratives rarely venture far down the vertical axis – involving no more (necessarily) than describing an *institutional* arrangement for the pursuit of the rights in question in the form a draft or framework convention.

For example, 'environmental constitutionalism' as a strategy to consolidate adjudicatory gains in environmental rights and communicate them into the transnational arena is largely declaratory in character (Kotzé 2015). Whether in its 'thin' form (providing only an architecture of environmental governance) or in its 'thick' version (announcing fundamental values and higher-order principles), it is long on aspiration, conceptual invention, and affective appeal – occasionally descending close enough to earth to provide general comments about potential institutional arrangements that might fit its bill. The main direction of movement, however, is clearly from aspirational description, through the identification of new environmental and human rights concepts, to the hoped-for behavioral result of new (or increased) environmental rights motivation. If there is an endemic weakness in this form of narrative, it would be its ethereal quality. Even its admirers regard it as always "a work in progress, asymptomatically striving toward an unattainable but undeniable goal of universal recognition and respect" (Kysar 2010, 245). Although this is more than sufficient to warm the scholarly heart, it is likely to leave both environmental and human rights activists with a distinct chill.

The adjudicatory rights model, in its narrative form, follows the same horizontal axis of Table 1, but at the most concrete level of the narrative map. Specific *material* conditions that significantly disadvantage vulnerable parties (damages) are identified and their character as harmful *outcomes* for fundamentally important interests of the parties (causation) are alleged in the most forceful language possible. The ultimate objective is to place the existing circumstances of the represented parties in such a *critical* light that the conscience of the 'court' to whom the narrative is addressed (be it judicial or administrative) is so shocked that denial of the requested relief is rendered impossible. At this stage, the adjudicatory narrative must usually provide a *strategic* supplement – showing the court how the relief being sought can be provided effectively and within the bounds of the court's existing behavioral repertoire. This generally requires a foray into the less concrete terrain of arguably related precedent or suitably pliable statutory language. If the advocate has made their case with sufficient persuasiveness, this somewhat more abstract step should be relatively easy for a court to take (especially if a relevant and successful example of prior regulatory experience can be provided).

Taking another example from the level of the nation-state (where environmental human rights are now mostly asserted and acquitted), after decades of inaction by elected officials, litigation brought by ordinary citizens (based on the concept of a general right to a healthy environment and the severity of the grievances of which they complained) provoked the Philippine Supreme Court to order twelve government agencies to develop a comprehensive plan to clean up the water of Manila Bay. The agencies were given six months to produce the plan, and were also required to undertake a wide range of remedial and preventative measures (Boyd 2012). Taking a strategic turn up the behavioral path, the court also "adopted the extraordinary remedy of continuing mandamus, giving itself the power to supervise implementation of the restoration plan" (169).

This new juxtaposition of declaratory and adjudicatory human rights (as narratives) allows us to at least imagine these traditions working in tandem – as mutually reinforcing efforts related to a particular environmental concern – rather than serially, or even in patterns of interference (as when the prospect of litigation is used to frighten decision-makers away from proposals for new rights). Table 3 represents this new relationship in graphic form. Although this revised conceptual framework offers the hopeful prospect of achieving greater synergy between the declaratory and adjudicatory models, it also poses new challenges to effective human rights advocacy. If these two models make only limited efforts to close the gap between them, by venturing only one step up or down the scale of abstraction, the opportunities for coordination (or even simply mutual comprehension) are similarly limited. Without the broader *explanatory* link between its critical and strategic efforts and their potential affective benefits, the adjudicatory model falls short of the more comprehensive behavioral changes to which it might reasonably aspire – by (for instance) depriving nonstate actors of the understanding of how significant a role they can play, even in areas as complex as international

Table 3 A normative-analytic map of human rights narratives

Level/reflexivity	Descriptive	Cognitive	Behavioral
Most abstract	↓ *Aspirational* →	*Inputs* →	*Affective*
	Institutional	Throughput	Explanatory
	Programmatic	Outputs	**Strategic**
Most concrete	**Material** →	**Outcomes** →	**Critical** ↑

Declaratory narratives (in italics) – the universal declaration approach – declare and justify.
Deliberative narratives – the recursive discourse approach – coordinate and institutionalize.
Adjudicatory narratives (in bold) – the rights revolution approach – 'litigate' and consolidate.

environmental governance (Green 2014). And the declaratory approach to human rights seems habitually to fall short precisely where *programmatic* change (implementation) is needed to convert its aspirational and institutional innovations into concrete material benefits – largely for reasons of strategic gamesmanship that have long been understood by political scientists (Bardach 1978).

Perhaps of even greater importance, the cognitive heartland of this map largely remains terra incognita. A clear implication of the analytical framework represented in Table 3 is that the cognitive aspect of human rights narratives is neglected (to a significant extent) by both the declaratory and adjudicatory traditions. To the extent that this problem exists, it results from more than the conceptual observation that declaratory human rights efforts tend to be abstract and that adjudicatory approaches tend to be concrete in their orientation. It also results from what is, perhaps, a more temperamental matter – that some human rights advocates strongly believe that language matters because words have inherent power while others care more deeply about what people do than about their rhetoric. This may explain (at least in part) why declaratory and adjudicatory narratives often fail to "turn the corner" any further than they do – why declarations rarely extend description beyond basic institutional concerns and adjudication rarely pursues behavioral change into abstract issues of explanation and attitude.

With these conceptual and temperamental tendencies in mind, what sorts or narratives might one imagine filling the cognitive territory between declaration and adjudication? A valid way to characterize this mid-range sort of narrative is that they need to be deliberative – that is to say, narratives of a discursive (rather than authoritative or imperative) character that rely on practical theorizing from the best available evidence and the testing of general maxims against the demands of particular cases (Baber and Bartlett 2005). Although this is precisely the kind of prudential reasoning that in the hands of some gave casuistry a bad name (Jonsen and Toulmin 1990), it need not degenerate into sophistry. When practiced by the parties to a disagreement or those facing a common problem under conditions of authenticity and mutual respect (rather than by detached and potentially cynical observers), narratives of this sort will tend to go no farther than the facts will take them, suspend judgment on matters that are significantly in doubt, and hold to their conclusions only so long as they continue to be supported by experience.

If this is the narrative form that we need to complete our repertoire of environmental rights narratives, where are we likely to find those narratives? Or, perhaps more accurately, who might we expect to find advancing those narratives? In his early treatment of the subject, Epp (1998) concentrated on the roles of civil rights lawyers, community activists, and judges in getting the rights revolution in the United States started. This analysis provides a rich description of what we have characterized here as an adjudicatory narrative. A decade later, however, Epp (2009) refocused his attention on the cooperation between civil society actors and regulatory bureaucrats in creating what he characterized as "the legalistic state." Epp described examples of activists and professionals using legal liability, lawsuit-generated publicity, and innovative managerial ideas to pursue the implementation of new rights. These strategies, pursued by networks of advocates with varying but complementary backgrounds, produce rights frameworks designed to make institutions accountable through intricate rules, employee training, and managerial oversight. According to Epp, such practices are becoming ubiquitous across bureaucratic organizations, replacing litigation with anticipatory regulation that rarely requires new legislation. While the headlines may go to the declarations of politicians and diplomats, or the courtroom exploits of crusading litigators, the deliberative strategies of interest *coordination* and gradual *institutionalization* are the means by which rights are made real.

Deliberative Narratives of Environmental Rights: Exploring a New Territory

Another real-world illustration will permit grasping more fully the potential of this "map" of environmental rights narratives. Consider the experience of the residents of the area surrounding the Mapungubwe National Park and the Mapungubwe Cultural Landscape, a UNESCO World Heritage site since 2003. The entire Mapungubwe region of South Africa's Limpopo Province is an area of great historical and cultural importance to the South African people. It is also an area of immense economic value because of its resource extraction potential. Although the region's diamond mining features most highly in the popular imagination, our interest is in the problems presented by its coal mining activities.

When an Australian company, Coal of Africa, Limited (CoAL), was licensed to conduct both open pit and underground coal mining nearby, the residents of Mapungubwe were limited in the ability to defend their environmental rights by the imbalance of power and resources that is typical to these cases. They enjoyed the benefit of statutorily favorable circumstances, but a concerted campaign of litigation to acquit those nominal rights was in practical terms out of the question. As with human rights issues generally, the environmental rights problems posed by CoAL's proposed mining activities would place the local population at a severe disadvantage (relative to the mining firm) in terms of litigation resources. Beyond this general difficulty, the Mapungubwe communities faced challenges particular to the defense of environmental rights.

These included "the small window of time available in which to take action" before irremediable environmental damage occurred, the difficulty in "quantifying environmental harm" for a court in the same way that businesses can quantify the potential economic damages of granting relief, the problem of securing expert advice and testimony in an industry-dominated knowledge community, and the challenge of making technical data intelligible to a court (Chamberlain 2017, 12).

But the Mapungubwe communities were able to secure the assistance of the Centre for Applied Legal Studies and the Centre for Environmental Rights at the University of Witwatersrand. This dual representation allowed the area's residents to file a number of administrative challenges to the series of regulatory decisions that mining projects of this sort always involve. This strategy, of course, has a cost-levying effect that makes it both a standard tactic for environmentalists and a predictable cost of doing business for industry. More important, however, this community was able to go beyond the adjudicatory strategies that so often fail to protect both the environment and human rights. An innovative network of determined local activists and dedicated regulatory administrators – held together both by their own commitment and by the creative efforts of university-based legal advocates – were able to craft a strategy that combined populism and professionalism in an especially promising way.

The populist face of the Mapungubwe strategy consisted of community learning exchanges (CLEs). This technique takes account of the fact that a serious deficit of information lies at the heart of the power imbalance between rural communities and resource extraction industries. As a consequence, the equality of information that is an essential precondition of fair agreement "is not present in engagements between mining companies and communities" (Chamberlain 2017, 9). Community members are easily misled about the likely benefits and possible costs of the development proposed for their region. But a community learning exchange introduces members of a community likely to be affected by a proposed mining project with residents in an area where mining development has already taken place. CLEs also allow communities to pool their understanding of and information regarding the threats to their environmental rights and to present that information to others in more systematic and sophisticated ways. Enabling CLEs is a task at which nongovernmental organizations (NGOs) and legal advocates (especially those with strong social science skill sets) should be particularly adept. They must, of course, respect the moral and political agency of the communities whose rights they seek to protect. An astute and self-aware combination of the expertise of civil society and the legal profession should be able to show that respect, while advancing the environmental rights of politically vulnerable groups and individuals.

The importance of professionalism to effective environmental rights advocacy is especially evident in the second major component of the Mapungubwe strategy – collaborative compliance monitoring. Public participation in environmental monitoring has long been known to contribute to increasing the knowledge on the state of the environment at the same time it promotes citizens' involvement in environmental protection. The usefulness of voluntarily collected data, however, is often limited in its influence due to a lack of confidence in data collection procedures. Additionally, data quality is often unknown and the data are usually dispersed and nonstructured. Information and communication technologies may promote the use of voluntary collected data through the development of a collaborative system that incorporates tools and methodologies to facilitate data collection, access, and validation (Gouveia et al. 2004). Still, regulatory decision-makers are reluctant to rely on information whose provenance they regard as suspect. In the case of Mapungubwe, however, this problem was addressed by the establishment of a special body (the Vele Colliery Environmental Management Committee), which was mandated and overseen by the terms of the licenses granted by the South African Department of Water Affairs and Department of Environmental Affairs (Chamberlain 2017). On the committee sat both national and provincial administrative officials, local municipalities and state agencies, farmers' unions and "for the first time in the history of the mining industry in South Africa: civil society" (11). The effective involvement of civil society actors as defenders of environmental rights was made possible in this instance by the representation (and guidance) that they enjoyed from the University of Witwatersrand-based Centre for Applied Legal Studies and the Centre for Environmental Rights – which was able to conceive of a way to make the UNESCO World Heritage framework perform the functions of a nonexistent international regime on environmental human rights.

This dual strategy of populist professionalism maps onto our analytical framework in ways that reveal the discursive middle range of environmental rights narratives (Table 4). A 'programmatic' information initiative (community learning) helps communities to recognize threats to environmental rights as the result of authoritative actions (outputs) of regulatory officials rather than isolated events. This new cognitive perspective is both inherently critical (because it problematizes regulatory decisions) and productive of a deeper understanding of the decision-making process (throughput) by which regulatory decision-makers convert cognitive inputs (the assertion of demands and offers of support) into authoritative action. This improved cognitive circumstance provides explanatory power to communities who seek to assert their environmental rights that both enhances their ability to change the affective environment of their struggle and helps them to refine the strategies they use to pursue their aims.

Table 4 The discursive middle range of environmental rights

Level / Reflexivity	Descriptive	Cognitive	Behavioral
Most abstract	*Aspirational*	*Inputs*	*Affective*
	Institutional	Throughput →	Explanatory ↕
	Programmatic →	Outputs ↑	**Strategic**
Most concrete	**Material**	**Outcomes**	**Critical** ↑

Declaratory narratives (in italics) – the universal declaration approach – declare and justify.
Deliberative narratives – the recursive discourse approach – coordinate and institutionalize.
Adjudicatory narratives (in bold) – the rights revolution approach – 'litigate' and consolidate.

This analysis clearly suggests that an especially effective form of environmental advocacy can be achieved when: (1) communities where environmental rights are at risk can be reached by environmental NGOs that help them both to understand their circumstances more clearly and organize to pursue their interests more effectively; (2) those NGOs can secure the services of legal advocacy possessed of an appropriate social scientific skill set to sharpen community-based rights narratives and ground them empirically; and (3) the imperatives produced by community organizing and legal advocacy are focused on key regulatory actors in a way that improves the protection of substantive environmental rights by enhancing procedural environmental rights.

A second implication of this analysis is rather more sobering. There is no reason to believe that threats to the environmental rights of human communities will ever require anything less than bespoke strategies like those developed in the Mapungubwe region of South Africa. A one-size-fits-all approach to the problem seems to be completely implausible. By the same token, threats to environmental rights are so ubiquitous in the modern world that chasing one ad hoc solution after another would seem to be a Sisyphean task – given that new threats arise almost daily and that solutions to the problems that they pose seem rarely to be permanent. So how can we imagine this sort of local success spreading? To borrow (and reverse) a traditional slogan from the environmental movement, how can we begin to do better thinking locally and acting globally?

Daunting as this challenge may be, it is perfectly possible to describe in general terms what a transnational response to this challenge would look like. If the proper combination of legal and social scientific scholarship and advocacy skill could be seeded in one nation after another (and in subnational regions in larger states), those organizational nodes would be capable of institutionalizing the process of building what would otherwise be one-off environmental rights coalitions. Although it would not be an essential element of the strategy, it is easiest to imagine these organizing nodes at universities (as was the case in the Mapungubwe). Not only is that where the coincidence of legal and social scientific skill is most likely to occur, it is also where institutional resources and professional incentive structures would both allow for and encourage work of this sort. An information network among these organizing nodes would allow their successes (and setbacks) to become an environmental rights database of the sort that supports both basic social scientific research and the more applied work of legal restatement. Whether or not those new lines of innovation eventually produced formal international accords might well prove to be irrelevant. They might eventually constitute an environmental jus cogens that would take on a self-sustaining, even contractual, character (Weatherall 2015).

Be that as it may, much preliminary work remains to be done before Mapungubwe-style strategies can aspire to transnational application. Linking the declaratory and adjudicatory models of environmental rights through narratives of the discursive middle range will require us to understand in far more detail the terrain that this mapping exercise urges us to explore. Across a wide range of substantive environmental challenges, and the environmental rights that they threaten, we need to judge the lay of the land so that plausible courses across it can be charted. Just how great is the distance between the declaratory and the adjudicatory? What obstacles lie in-between and what resources are available to overcome them? Perhaps most important, how many different versions of these answers will we eventually need? This preliminary work falls into (at least) four basic categories.

First, across a useful range of substantive environmental rights, we need to describe in significant detail precisely what international support for environmental rights currently exists in international law. In principle, it is not difficult to describe a test for determining the existence of a rule in any area of international law. "First, the decision-making elites in states must perceive the rule to be authoritative . . . second, the rule must be controlling. It must be reflected in the actual practice of states" (Arend 1999). In practice, of course, matters are not so simple. States may claim to recognize a rule as authoritative and may offer a range of accounts of how their behavior comports with that rule. Perversely enough, the more fundamental the rule (as with rights), the more likely it is that violations will be disguised as some variant of compliance. There have been notable recent attempts to advance an omnibus substantive environmental rights regime, falling into two categories. One is aspirational, such as a proposed framework regime that consists of changes to the existing international legal architecture intended to better protect the environment and human environmental interests (Turner 2014). The other category is more analytical than aspirational, comprising the development of legal principles intended to reflect actual or emerging international human rights law, for example, the rights of children "to life, health, development, an adequate standard of living, play and recreation" (Knox 2018, 9)

Second, across this same range of substantive environmental rights, we need to discover (in so far as we can) whether or not sufficient popular support for progress in these areas exists (or can be developed) at the global level. In some instances, we may be able to begin to answer this question with comparative polling data. When quantitative evidence is available, it should be used to its best effect. The absence of such data in particular cases – even data suggesting a relative lack of support – cannot by itself be dispositive. People around the world, living and working in different religious and judicial traditions, have eventually found "reasons to support various human rights instruments" that did not originally appeal to them because they came to see that those instruments "embody protections that they both want and need" (Appiah 2005, 260).

Third, we must determine whether such congruence as we can discover between elite and popular opinion actually constitutes a workable consensus (or merely papers over continuing disagreement with empty rhetoric). It is not unusual to encounter circumstances in which official pronouncements and public opinion polls seem to be in substantial agreement, and yet little of substance has resulted. The challenge, when that phenomenon occurs, is to distinguish between circumstances in which people (presumably politicians) are dissembling and when a congruence of opinion has not produced environmentally friendly results for other reasons. Environmental rights, both substantive and procedural, should enhance rather than foreclose democratic debate. In a democratic polity, the point of these rights is (arguably) to "create environmental due process that minimizes judicial involvement and broadens democratic processes" by improving the "conditions and inclusiveness of dialogue by redressing major power imbalances in political communication and representation" (Eckersley 2004, 137). Human rights evolve, and new rights emerge, but not merely because they are socially constructed or because experience demonstrates the need for them. Equally, if not more important, is that "human rights grow and evolve as the human relationships from which they emerge change the ways in which we relate to each other, our politics, and our natural world" (Hiskes 2009, 146). Therefore, deeper understanding of how those involved in rights-related environmental actions understand themselves and their own narratives will be increasingly critical.

Fourth, and finally, we must find ways to anticipate how the rights we hope to advocate will be received by humanity's varying legal traditions (and their constituent administrative institutions). How will any normative consensus we think we may have found play – in Peoria (and Phuket, and Petrozavodsk, and Pretoria, and Port-au-Prince)? Beginning with the adoption of the UN

Universal Declaration of Human Rights in 1948, there was a period of "unchallenged dominance of a rights discourse in humanitarian affairs" during which countries that routinely violated the most basic rights of their own citizens also "paid lip service to the basic idea of human rights." Eventually, however, human rights "came under challenge from a communitarian 'Asian values' discourse, which characterized individual values as a Western construct" (Dryzek 2010, 183). Thus began a time when the Western world became increasingly reluctant to forcefully advocate "one of its greatest cultural achievements" – the very concept of individual human rights, as codified in the Universal Declaration and other fundamental political documents (Cliteur 2010, 138). To make matters still worse, after 2001, the West's commitment to its own rights discourse "was weakened by the rise of a discourse of counterterror that prioritized the prevention of terrorism over the protection of rights" (Dryzek 2010, 183).

This final challenge may be our most daunting, as well as the one that it is most important for us to meet. One might imagine that – in spite of the manifestly social construction of nature that varies strikingly – the very objectivity of the physical environment would cause thinking about our relationship to it to converge across cultures. Even failing that, the assumption that Western liberalism is especially eco-friendly is questionable. For example, an argument can certainly be made that Confucian personalism, family ideals, and social conscience "have much to offer the contemporary world, and in key respects may provide a better grounding for both human rights and environmental rights" (De Bary and Tu 1998, 9). Perhaps of greatest importance, the conflation of diversity and disagreement is simply erroneous. In fact, "arguments tend to be the most intense and numerous among people who share a lot of their ideational and normative tenets" and, moreover, "there are fruitful kinds of disagreement that you can have only if you share all sorts of previous founding assumptions" (Appiah 2005, 255). If we dwell on that observation, even only briefly, two conclusions immediately suggest themselves. One is that there is no reason to believe, a priori, that cultural, religious, and social diversity will prevent us from coming to broad transnational conclusions about the environmental rights we all share merely as a result of our shared humanity. Second, the fact that many of our most fruitful disagreements are only possible if we share a firm foundation of basic assumptions should encourage us to continue the search for conceptions of human rights that we can all *declare*.

The results of that search will never satisfy those who disparage the Universal Declaration as "an embarrassment" because it has "either had no effect on the behavior of states or very little" (Posner 2009, 185–186). Even without challenging the dubious empiricism of such claims, it is certainly possible to sustain an argument (as previewed here) that declaratory rights narratives move humanity in an identifiable and positive direction and, with the proper linking narratives, can eventually transform the human condition through both the democratization of regulatory processes and the expansion of environmental rights doctrines via adjudicatory change. That is why it is important to try to anticipate how environmental rights narratives might be received by humanity's varying legal traditions and to better understand how future environment rights as a subset of human rights generally might, by emergent global consensus or near-consensus, become established as real, meaningful rights. Likewise, under-standing how a networked advocacy of environmental rights might succeed in advancing an environmental rights agenda in any given political context should suggest (at least in general terms) how such advocacy will have to diverge from our ideal-typical account of it.

4 Regimes, Restatements, and Rights: Charting a Post-National Course for Consensus

What paths are possible and "least unlikely" for the evolution of a global consensus on a set of environmental human rights?

With regard to the possibility of negotiating an international agreement that provides for a right of all individuals to a healthy environment, there is both warrant for this objective and guidance for pursuing it. Already available for consideration are both a 'checklist' for the effort in the form of draft frame-work principles (Knox 2018) and a fully fleshed-out version of what such a treaty might look like (Turner 2014). It takes nothing away from either effort to point out the improbability of gaining, in the near future, the necessary support (particularly from the more powerful countries) for any such an agreement because both authors are fully aware of the long odds. It is no more a criticism of their work than it is a concession that environmental human rights will remain out of reach by this approach because the conventional mechanisms of international environmental governance (negotiation of new multilateral environmental agreements) are unlikely to secure them any time soon.

A second way that a consensus on environmental human rights could emerge and become entrenched is through their inclusion or discovery in more general, often already existing, human rights treaties and 'soft law' declarations and the processes of interpreting and applying. The UN Human Rights Council com-missioned a 'mapping report' that indicated where existing human rights agreements touch on concerns of international environmental governance either explicitly or implicitly (Knox 2013). This map covers much territory, and usefully so. But the request for the project is an implicit admission that both general human rights treaties and international environmental agreements are woefully inadequate for the protection of environmental human rights (and that they are likely to remain so).

A third approach is to finish the job of declaring a substantive environmental right in every national constitution – that is, to continue on a path of creating a multinational system of environmental human rights. The world is already more than halfway there, and Boyd (2012) documents over 130 examples of how that success can happen. Undoubtedly, these declaratory successes harvested the lowest-hanging fruit. Yet nothing succeeds like success – and such a multinational approach allows the focus of international resources (the International Monetary Fund, the World Bank, civil society, academic study) in a small arena (a few countries at a time). A sufficiently broad but unformalized agreement on the subject among nations could eventually provide a customary international law solution in the form of substantive environmental human rights that international tribunals will respect. An international environmental human rights treaty may never be necessary, or it might be adopted as merely a formal recognition and codification of already established rights.

The prospects and potential for all three of these approaches, separately or together, to evolve in the direction of establishing real environmental human rights might be greater if the processes of policy consensus were better understood. First, building on but going beyond theoretical and analytical work on consensus in environmental politics and earth system governance (Baber and Bartlett 2015), we require more insight into how international regime formation and the creation of national law relate (or might conceivably relate) to one another in any given policy space. Second, we need to better understand how human rights can operate as summary statements of historical, social, and political consensus. This will allow us to tie the descriptive, cognitive, and behavioral functions of human rights identified in Section 3 more directly to the various substantive forms that an environmental human rights consensus can take. Third, we must develop a better appreciation of how any consensus that substantive environmental human rights provisions represent can contribute to earth system governance at both the national and international levels.

If the recognition of a body of rights is genuinely necessary to the extended practice of global democracy, then earth system governance processes can move in the direction of becoming more democratic and more environmentally benign by fostering the establishment of environmental human rights. Like all human rights, environmental human rights should be understood as constituting the bounds of legitimate democratic discourse. But if such rights are never a gift – not from God, or Nature, or philosophers, or judges, or parliaments, or international conferences – what are the kinds of political and social processes that can lead to their establishment? Although policy norm diffusion, and even human rights norm diffusion

(Keck and Sikkink 2014, Sikkink 1998), is reasonably well studied, international institutional uptake (Goodin and Dryzek 2006) is less well understood.

The processes of regime formation and legal restatement exemplify and render more concrete the characterization of rights narratives as descriptions of areas of normative consensus – of places in the political world where we have adopted a 'final vocabulary' in order to terminate the otherwise infinite regress of normative justification. The formation of international regimes and the tradition of legal restatement are processes similar to each other, animated by the same desire to document areas in which a broad consensus about the legitimate and desirable ends of public policy might exist. In this regard, the idea and implications of consensus matter. A broad and enhanced analysis of consensus from the perspectives of history, sociology, and political science suggests how reimagined versions of the processes of international regime formation and legal restatement can effectively serve the cause of extending both human rights and environmental narratives, such that they would be more likely to complement and reinforce one another.

Regimes and Restatements: Moving the Environmental Rights Discourse Forward

When a group of nations initiate the process of international regime formation, they commonly do so with some form of declaration – asserting their agreement to a general principle that they believe all nations should respect in their relationships with one another. As strongly as this conviction might be held in any individual state, its meaning elsewhere in the world is always a subject for debate. But if a sufficient number of states can begin the process of fleshing out an abstract normative judgment on which they believe they agree without discovering insurmountable areas of unanticipated disagreement in the process, a framework (or constitutive) agreement is often the result. If the developmental process continues long enough and successfully enough, regulatory standards are adopted. As this process continues, the meaning of the underlying normative principles becomes increasingly clear as their potential applications to real-world challenges of governance are discussed and the anticipated consequences are weighed. The hoped-for result is a regime of sufficient concreteness that it can actually serve as a guide to human action – perhaps even the basis for future enforcement measures.

Whereas the process of international regime formation is *deductive*, beginning with an abstract principle and spelling out its concrete meaning, the process of legal restatement is far more *inductive*. It begins with a large collection of legal solutions to a set of closely related problems and attempts to infer from those solutions what the operative normative principle(s) is (must be). If that restatement is well received by the legal community – that is, if that community judges it to state the law in a useful way that allows actors to conform their behavior to it and to resolve any disputes that may arise in relatively predictable ways – the restatement will gain credibility. If its credibility rises to a sufficient level, and if doctrinal uniformity is of sufficient importance in the area of legal practice that it addresses, a restatement may provide the foundational material for the creation of a model code. Codes of that sort can (especially in federal systems of government) eventually result in the adoption of national legal regimes intended to memorialize in law the normative principles that arose from the corpus of litigation that provided the raw material for the restatement in the first instance. If that area of practice is sufficiently sensitive to international issues (trade and investment, environmental protection, human rights, and so forth), it may lead the state involved to propose international standards that are consistent with its own normative perspective. The barest outline of a similar process can be seen internationally, as adjudication and ongoing mutual adjustments beyond the state can lead to treatises and commissions that identify commonalities and best practices, which are then recommended back to states for consideration. These activities can push along the very slow and incremental process of development of customary law and endorsement of general principles. In turn, a regime may form around this gradual reification and may inspire the drafting of formal treaties.

A graphic representation of this process, and its possible relationship to the process of international regime formation, is summarized in Figure 1.

The merits of this representation are several. First, it elaborates on our description of the relationship of the models of human rights narratives identified in Section 3 (the declaratory and the adjudicatory). Second, the juxtaposition of national and international norm-building processes suggests many avenues of possible scholarly exploration – particularly for those whose interests lie mainly in the analysis of governance narratives and how they are received in various legal cultures. Third, this way of understanding the relationship between national and international governance norms provides a handy map of the governance terrain – showing (as a general matter) how to chart a course from the most concrete and immediate concerns, through the process of creating and deploying political consensus, to a destination where a need shared by all humanity may eventually be addressed in a just and equitable manner. Fourth, it provides insight into both the Janus-faced role played by elected officials (in ratifying domestic norm-building and initiating its international equivalent) and the reasons why those officials and the states they serve will remain salient even in an era of

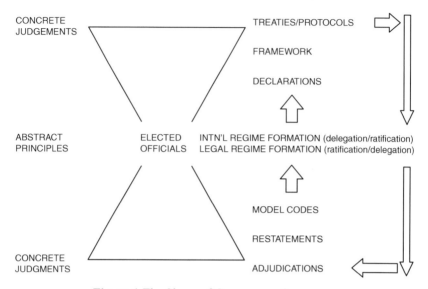

Figure 1 The Shape of Governance Consensus

globalization. This representation of global norm-building, does not, however, answer all the questions that might reasonably be of concern and it raises some new ones that might not have otherwise occurred. Why does consensus (as opposed to mere compromise) matter so much and will it bear the weight that rights, restatement, and regimes place on it? How does conceiving legal restatement and regime formation as related processes – potentially even as one continuous process – empower us to pursue environmental and human rights objectives more effectively?

Why Consensus Matters

'Consensus' is a rich and multifaceted concept, but considered simply as a word, it is a sadly limited thing – especially when compared with its cousin 'compromise'. Whereas compromise occurs in English as both a verb and a noun, consensus is a noun only. Moreover, compromise, even as a noun, has more typical senses of meaning than does consensus. A compromise can be a mutual promise, a joint agreement, an arbitrated settlement, a pattern of concessions, a pragmatic adjustment, an exposure to risk, or merely the midpoint in a distribution of values. In the world of dictionary definitions, consensus is merely general agreement or the collective opinion by consent of some number of persons. As late as 1940, the word consensus occurred only rarely in English. But the postwar years saw a dramatic increase in the incidence of 'consensus' in English, notably in the United States. How can we account for such a dramatic rise in the incidence of the word 'consensus' and why should we care?

Consensus in History

One reason that use of the word 'consensus' may have increased so markedly in the mid-1900s is that some especially loquacious humans became enamored of the concept shortly after World War II. Chief among these was a group of American historians who are often referred to as counter-progressives. The timing of this development is subject to several explanations. Historians were as appalled as all reasonable humans at the carnage that had been inflicted by humanity upon itself over differences of ideology and interest and, thus, may have turned their attention to commonalities. It may be true as well that the impending threat of the Cold War put pressure (either conscious or unconscious) on some historians to find an account of history that could serve as a uniting force for the free world in its confrontation with communism. Both these influences – when combined with the sense that progressive scholars had overemphasized polarized conflict and cyclical discontinuities – probably made a consensus-oriented reaction against prewar historical scholarship almost inevitable (Grob and Billias 2000).

In order to understand why a consensus-orientation became so compelling for historians once it had emerged, it is useful to look more closely at some of the specific components that made up the consensus perspective and gave rise in the United States to a broad commitment to the idea of an American Consensus as a descriptive model for telling the American story. There is, amusingly enough, a lack of consensus among consensus historians about the character of this American consensus. All argue, in general terms, that the unifying force of a common culture (rather than the divisive influence of class) has been the determining factor in American history. Hartz (1955) attributed the social solidarity enjoyed by Americans to the fact that, although they are a strongly ideological people, they agree on the same ideology to a remarkable degree. Hartz characterized this broadly conceived and abstractly articulated agreement on ideology as the "American Way of Life" (1955). The specifics of this ideology were relatively simple – private property, individualism, popular sovereignty, and natural rights.

The American belief in *private property* is, as a general matter, unremarkable. It would be hard to find a political culture anywhere in the developed world that allows no room for personal possessions. But private property (and in particular the private ownership of the means of production) becomes a highly salient political concept when it is united with a commitment to *individualism*. When so conjoined, these concepts give rise to a belief that *entrepreneurship* is both the foundation of a successful society and an important source of social cohesion – in short, a basis for consensus. Thus, Hofstadter (1979) wrote that his view of consensus had its genesis in his effort to make sense of the Marxism of the 1930s. He eventually concluded that reform movements had never been of fundamental importance in America, and had never become radical, because they were basically struggles by small capitalists against big capitalists (in an effort to become big capitalists themselves).

The idea of *popular sovereignty* plays a role in consensus history similar to that of entrepreneurship. Belief in democratic rule, in spite of the fact that it is subject to a variety of interpretations, is seen as an essential element of the American way and a major source of social cohesion. The most interesting account of this is the scholarship of Hartz (1964), who analyzed the emergence of Australia, Canada, Latin America, South Africa, and the United States from the political culture of Europe through a process of fragmentation. In this process, an ideological fragment of European culture detached itself from the whole to become the central organizing principle of a new society. In the American case, a bourgeois-liberal fragment of seventeenth-century British society became the foundation of a political culture that was far narrower in scope than its parent and, for that reason, more cohesive and consensual.

Supporting both entrepreneurship and popular sovereignty, according to consensus historians, was a broad agreement in America about the existence and importance of certain *natural rights*. This orientation toward rights may not, however, be as promising as it sounds. For instance, Hofstadter (1979, 454) draws a distinction between what he refers to as "policy consensus" on the one hand and a thinner "constitutional consensus" on the other. It is within the context created by this distinction that Hartz (1955) could speak of a system of democracy wherein ideology was of no importance. This system works, he concedes, only by virtue of certain processes that its theory never describes and to which, in fact, its theory is actually hostile in important ways. These processes include group coercion, crowd psychology, economic privilege, and a conflict of interests from which an equilibrium roughly representing the public interest emerges. For Hartz, apparently, it is primarily an agreement to participate in (or acquiesce in the results of) this political game that constitutes the political element of the American consensus.

Empirical studies on these matters have long revealed an ambivalent and contradictory set of American attitudes toward the rights customarily associated with democracy. These investigations suggest that there is substantial agreement on abstract democratic principles but very limited agreement on the application of those principles to the substantive concerns associated with concrete cases. This gap is particularly noticeable, and troublesome, with respect to the democratic rights of disfavored minorities (Klosko 2000). Suffice it to say, the ability of the human rights of individuals (as humans) to survive the rights-based individualism of the American consensus probably depends on the ability of political elites (who are often found to be more solicitous of individual rights than Americans generally) to appeal to American values in the abstract while avoiding or reframing the specific limitations imposed upon individuals (particularly those who constitute political majorities) by the often contradictory character of precisely those same values.

For a perspective so well suited to its era, consensus history enjoyed a remarkably short time in the sun. The first major criticism of consensus history proved to be devastating. Higham's (1959) accusation that the counter-progressives were trying to "homogenize our history" by writing discontent and conflict out of the American experience opened a floodgate of criticism – which flowed all the more strongly coming at the same time when a sociocultural upheaval was beginning to rend the fabric of the American consensus. Some critics argued that even though consensus history might explain why the United States avoided some forms of conflict, it cannot explain why it suffered from others. Another complaint was that consensus history, whatever its merits in the areas where it can be applied, blinds Americans to the facts of their past (urban poverty, southern racism, etc.) that suggest persistent cultural heterogeneity. These and other failings of consensus history resulted in its confinement to a far narrower range of historical questions than the theory's authors aspired to address (Sternsher 1975).

When one examines the circumstances of life in postwar America, the motivations for a consensus theory of history are evident. Consensus history, while a descriptive model, was far more than a label for a preferred reality. It carried with and within itself a self-conscious hope for a better society. It is unsurprising that this same impulse would drive the postwar work of at least some scholars in the field of sociology in their search for a *cognitive* (as opposed to descriptive) model to account for the American experience.

Consensus in Society

Although it could be argued that the consensus-oriented theory of society is as old as the work of Plato and Aristotle, it has particular importance to the search for environmental human rights during the same postwar time frame that bounded consensus theories of history. The phrase "consensus-conflict debate" in sociology is "of relatively recent origin and is commonly used to describe a controversy that arose in sociology in the 1950's, reached its peak around 1970, and has been declining since that time" (Bernard 1983, 2). Shils (1961, 1410) provided what is perhaps the most useful summary of consensus sociology. Modern society, especially in its latest phase, is "characteristically a consensual society" in which "personal attachments" loom large, and in which "the individual person is appreciated" and there is "concern for his well-being." For Shils, contemporary Western societies represented a new stage in human existence – a stage in which "consensus rests on individuality and on the bonds that can exist between individualities; not a consensus that assumes the absence of individuality and crushes its manifestations." Moreover, this new form of consensus had both social and political dimensions. It was "a consensus constructed out of the affectional ties of one individual for perceiving the individuality of another, out of a civility that perceives and attaches to the mere humanity of another person, out of a sense of nationality that perceives in the other the element of a shared territoriality" (1429).

As in the case of history, consensus sociology (commonly described as 'functionalism') is usually understood as standing in contradiction to a theoretical perspective that emphasizes conflict. Lipset (1975, 172) characterized the disagreement this way: "The focus by functionalists on 'values' as distinct from 'interests' seems to the critics to result in an underestimation of the inherent forces for social conflict among those having different interests." Again, as with history, Marx played a role in the debate between sociologists over consensus. "There can be little doubt that, as contrasted with Marxist analysis, with its predominant interest in change and conflict, functionalist sociology has devoted much more of its theoretical energies to explaining social order – the ways in which society is held together" (173). This fundamental difference of perspective was a dominant theme in sociology for decades. In fact, it is arguable that the conflict has never really been resolved – only partially outgrown in the finest pragmatist tradition – leaving a residual conflict–consensus debate that complicates sociological theory and limits our capacity to understand human rights.

Bernard (1983, 14) suggested that in understanding the debate over consensus, there are at least three important phenomena to be explored – three dimensions along which the human experience may be described as either consensual or conflictual. These dimensions, which track our fundamental concern over who we have been, who we are, and who we might become, are "*human nature, the contemporary state of society, and the ideal society*" (emphasis in original). Whether and to what extent human nature naturally inclines people to cooperate or compete is still unanswered. Suffice it to say, however, the issue is an essential element in any approach to understanding the human experience or explaining human behavior, as we can see from an examination of the work of Parsons (1951, 1961). In constructing his consensual (or functionalist) view of human nature, Parsons drew on elements of utilitarian, positivist, and idealist theory. From utilitarianism, he drew the argument that human beings are preeminently goal-oriented creatures. From the positivist tradition, he mined ideas about the situational character of human action – its dependence on various social, psychological, and biological factors. From idealism, Parsons drew the notion that ideas (in the form of beliefs, values, and norms) could also have a determining influence on human action. So the Parsonian individual is rationally motivated but also constrained by both situational conditions and social conventions. As a consequence, humans are always likely to be in search of cooperative arrangements to overcome their individual limitations as well as to gain the approbation of others in their choice of means to attain their goals.

Parsons's model of human nature is, of course, foundational for his view of a social system, which was any number of persons interacting with one another in pursuit of their goals, subject to some pattern of constraints, within a network of relations that is symbolically mediated in some way (1951, 5–6). Parsons discerned a consensual orientation that he described as "instrumental activism." This consensus was "more economic than political" and its goal orientation was "highly indefinite and pluralistic, being committed to a rather general direction of progress or improvement, without any clearly defined terminal goal" (1969, 206). Supporting this general consensus in every other well-ordered contemporary society was what Parsons described as its integrative subsystem. He called this subsystem "the societal community" (1971, 11), which refers to that aspect of a society (as a system of social systems) that serves as the focus for the solidarity of its members and as the consensual basis of its sustaining political integration.

Needless to say, the concept of a 'societal community' is at least as much normative as it is empirical. For the functionalist, it is not only a characteristic of any well-ordered contemporary society – it is an essential element of any society that a human being could rationally find desirable, for at least two reasons. First and foremost, the concept of the social community is grounded in societal values that are by definition conceptions of the desirable society as opposed to personal values that individuals might find appealing. Second, the social community exists as both a normative concept and an empirical fact. Therefore, a comparison of the actual to the possible is always implicit in it (Parsons 1971). As a particularly important example, the exclusion of groups who are resident within the territory of the society but whose values and aspirations find no expression within the social community suggests a shortcoming in any existing society. The ideal society would be the fully integrated society in which the values of all find expression and the cooperative arrangements for goal attainment are fully inclusive (1969). It would, in short, be based on a broadly held consensus about the acceptability of fundamental social institutions rather than a collection of historically contingent shared specificities (in effect, a *normative* form of diversity rather than a merely *aggregative* one).

In consensus (or functionalist) theory, systems of relative inequality or social stratification rest largely on agreements within given societies about positions, statuses, and roles – agreements regarding how social structures should be functionally understood, rather than merely described. The existence of a social community founded on widely shared values does not necessarily suggest a generally (much less uniformly) pacific social environment. Consensus sociologists view those deviant behaviors as localized dysfunctions that demonstrate the importance and vitality of the social consensus rather than threaten or cast doubt upon its existence. But if potentially disconfirming evidence is always entered into consensus sociology's ledger as an exception that proves the rule, then the theory's underlying rule is successfully insulated from virtually any empirical challenge.

In 1960, consensus sociologist Bell "announced the emergence of a consensus on the mixed economy and the halfway welfare state with the demise of the capitalism-versus-socialism conflict in the United States" (Sternsher 1975, 29). He characterized this development, perhaps too boldly, as the end of ideology (Bell 1960). To proclaim the end of ideology only a historical moment before campuses across the nation exploded with leftist fervor was, at the very least, unfortunate timing. It led to accusations that functionalist sociologists had made a concrete prediction that had been flatly contradicted by events and that their theoretical parochialism had blinded them to the most significant social developments of the time – one that was actually unfolding under their very noses (Kenniston 1975). Against what was, perhaps, the most aggressive criticisms aimed at their perspective, consensus sociologists' defense was that the existence of a normative consensus in society does not necessarily suggest cultural stagnation. A fairer reading of Bell, according to Lipset (1977), is that the grand humanistic ideologies of the nineteenth and early twentieth centuries had exhausted themselves and that future ideologies would be of a far more parochial and limited character. Lipset's second argument was that the student revolts of the sixties and early seventies were, in fact, expressions of just such a parochial viewpoint. The students, he argued, were not advancing a grand social vision, either new or old. Rather, they were reacting in a self-regarding but entirely predictable way to the increasing bureaucratization of higher education and the declining prospects for its graduates (Lipset 1979).

Regardless of how one chooses to adjudicate the dispute between consensus sociology and its critics, it would be hard to deny that structural-functionalism enjoyed a descriptive, explanatory, and predictive reach that consensus historians could only envy. Consensual sociology supplies more than just a model of human nature and a description of contemporary society. It provides both an analytical framework within which our collective future can be predicted and a normative yardstick by which our progress as a society can be measured. It is the capacity for prediction and appraisal, more than anything else, that explains the interest of a third collection of postwar scholars in the concept of consensus. These theorists are the consensus-oriented political scientists – whose hope was not to simply understand human society better, but to guide its behavior.

The 'Science' of Consensual Politics

As consensus historians and sociologists were developing their descriptive and cognitive theoretical constructs (mostly US-centric theorizing because only in America was a fantasy about an unforced national consensus seriously entertained), political scientists, both US and European, were peering intently over their shoulders. It is not unfair to characterize political scientists as members of a scavenger species, always on the lookout for a new theoretical titbit and, when found, often indifferent to its provenance. Somewhat more charitably, they might be described as intellectual Romans – constantly colonizing the territory of others under the banner 'The Politics of . . .' and adopting as their own the most valuable elements of the cultures that they invade. So when it came time to incorporate the work of consensus historians and sociologists into the canon of political science, in pursuit of *behavioral* approaches to collective action, the keepers of that tradition were more than ready.

Dahl's early study of local government (1961) concluded that that, even in small jurisdictions, public decisions were the result of interaction among a large collection of competing elites that, when looked at collectively, represented the polity in nearly all of its diversity. The outcome of this competition can never be taken for granted and no political decision is immune from later criticism and revision. But the evident agreement of all involved on the fundamental rules of the game convinced Dahl that Americans approached politics from a point of basic ideological consensus.

Dahl's understanding of this consensus emphasizes the importance of two core values that constitute the foundational premises of all democratic political orders: 'competition' (public contestation among various political actors) and 'participation' (defined with regard simply to the right to engage in the competition). From such a perspective, existing political systems can be graded based on the degree to which they possess these essential democratic elements and the stability of those systems can be predicted on that basis as well. Most modern political systems fall into a gray area, in that they are neither perfectly competitive nor inclusive: a dynamic equilibrium in a pluralistic and competitive system that Dahl came to call polyarchy (1972). A general acceptance of this polyarchic structure constitutes democracy's underlying social consensus.

Dahl was as concerned about the potentially disintegrative tendencies of social, political, and economic equality as any consensus historian or sociologist. He concluded that it is possible to achieve a society of real democracy and political equality without sacrificing liberty by extending democratic principles into the economic order. Although conceding that the idea of enterprise control by workers violates many conventional political and ideological assumptions of both corporate capitalism and state socialism, Dahl presented an empirically informed and philosophically acute defense of 'workplace democracy'. Experiences with economic democracy suggest that an economic system of worker-owned or worker-controlled enterprises could provide a much better foundation for democracy, political equality, and liberty than either our current system of corporate capitalism or the social alternatives that are popular on the left (Dahl 1986).

That the most prominent pluralist theorist of the last half of the twentieth century would advance such reasoning suggests something important for the consensualist perspective. It suggests that consensus is a more elastic concept than many of its early manifestations (and uses) would lead one to believe. Moreover, it holds out hope that consensus might reach beyond the abstract and 'constitutional' confines that Hofstadter and others had imposed on it. The possibility that consensus might be a realistic objective in at least some areas of policy-making under at least some circumstances has become a central concern for another group of political theorists who have contributed to the currency of that term – consociational democrats.

The leading theorist of consociational democracy is Lijphart, who began decades of research on consensus with an early study of the structural features of government in the Netherlands that have been used to bridge the cultural divides that complicate that country's politics (Lijphart 1976). The politics of the Netherlands has traditionally been characterized by a high commitment to the value of consensus. Lijphart's (1984) comparative study of the governmental structures of twenty-one democratic states found that, within the broad framework of democratic government, democratic states tend to cluster around two structural types: the *majoritarian* and *consensus* models. By use of these variables, Lijphart measured levels of majoritarian and consensus democracy for the twenty-one countries he examined. Although he found little difference in the actual performance of these two democratic types, Lijphart did find grounds to suggest that the consensus model is particularly suited to societies characterized by high levels of heterogeneity. He showed how consensus democracies have been able to develop political institutions that protect minorities and help mitigate political conflict in the face of high levels of pluralism. Where Dahl was able to describe the political culture that gives rise to societies that are both highly pluralistic and relatively stable, Lijphart added a valuable perspective on the political structures that are most appropriate to those societies.

A third group of political scientists, deliberative democrats, have provided a third perspective on political consensus – a description of the decision processes that might reasonably be expected to produce such consensus. Deliberative democracy (or discursive democracy) is a form of politics in which deliberation is central to collective choice. It frequently adopts elements of both consensus decision-making and majority rule, but it is never satisfied with the mere aggregation of existing preferences (which are taken to be variable rather than fixed). Deliberative democratic theory differs from traditional democratic theory in that authentic deliberation, not simple voting, is the primary source of legitimacy for processes of collective will formation.

Deliberative practices are generally compatible with both representative and direct forms of democracy. Some practitioners and theorists use the "deliberative" term to encompass any representative body whose members authentically deliberate on legislation without unequal distributions of power. Others restrict their use of the term exclusively to decision-making directly by lay citizens, as in direct democracy. Still others hold out the possibility that effective deliberative practices can combine both citizens and their representatives in the coproduction of governing norms.

For present purposes, the aspect of deliberative democracy that is of greatest interest is the role played in its theoretical justification by the idea of consensus. One of the deliberative democrat's fondest hopes is that "the deliberative process might produce consensus by actually changing minds through reasoned argument" (Baber and Bartlett 2005, 110). Deliberative democracy's leading theoretical figures, Rawls and Habermas, each featured consensus in their theoretical work.

Rawls is widely identified with his argument that "political liberalism looks for a political conception of justice" that can "gain the acceptance of an overlapping consensus of reasonable religious, philosophical, and moral doctrines" in the society that is to be regulated by that conception (Rawls 1993, 10). To arrive at that consensus, it is necessary to "find some point of view, removed from and not distorted by the particular features and circumstances" of social reality, a point of view "from which a fair agreement between persons regarded as free and equal can be reached" (23). Rawls (1971) referred to this point of view as the "original position" in which one would find oneself if blinded to one's own interests by a "veil of ignorance." In that position, Rawls assumes that each of us would seek solutions to political disagreements that would be agreed to in principle by rationally self-interested individuals who were unaware of how the resolution would affect them as individuals.

Habermas has a different (but complementary) view of consensus. He begins with the fundamental proposition that the "republican model of citizenship reminds us that constitutionally protected institutions of freedom are worth only what a population accustomed to political freedom and settled in the 'we' perspective of active self-determination makes of them" (Habermas 1996, 499). This premise does not mandate any particular decision-making process. It does, however, suggest that political decisions are rational in a democratic sense only if they are expressions of a general intent – that is, only if they *could have* come to pass under the ideal deliberative conditions that alone create legitimacy. Democratic society, therefore, is best envisioned as a "self-controlled learning process" (Baber and Bartlett 2005, 36). This requires adoption of decision processes that support the presumption that the fundamental institutions of a society and its basic political decisions would meet with "the unforced agreement of all of those involved, if they could participate, as free and equal, in a discursive will formation" (Habermas 1979, 186).

In comparing the orientations toward consensus of Rawls and Habermas, two observations are immediately possible. First, their views are in no critical way incompatible. Both assume that consensus will result from decision processes only if participants approach their task from an impartial perspective. Second, although compatible, the approaches of Rawls and Habermas emphasize different aspects of impartiality. Rawls focuses on the impartiality that results from rational ignorance, from the lack of information about how the decision at hand will affect one's own interests. Habermas, on the other hand, requires of us that we credit arguments in the decision process that are acceptable to all *despite* the fact that the participants know their interests (generally, because the arguments are grounded in intersubjectively reliable fact). In the first case, the decision-makers themselves are impartial and in the second case, it is the evidence presented to them that is impartial.

It is as though Rawls and Habermas had each noticed a different element of how juries operate in trials – Rawls has watched as voir dire has insured that no interested parties find their way onto the jury and Habermas has seen evidence ruled inadmissible because it cannot be relied upon by a conscientious decision-maker. One can easily imagine these requirements transposed into a consociational legislative context (à la Lijphart) in which the existence of mutually restraining minority vetoes promotes consensual outcomes. Only a little more imagination is required to conceive of a political culture in which the impartiality of decision processes and the consociational quality of governing institutions is so widely understood and appreciated that a genuine consensus about the legitimacy of the outcomes of the political system produces a high level of both consent to and support for social institutions generally.

Consensus in Regimes and Restatements: A Global Rights Foundation

The concept of consensus is of sufficient importance to merit a prominent position in our thinking about environmental human rights, particularly with regard to international regime formation and legal restatement. We began with the observation that the word 'consensus' occurs far more often in the English language than it used to. Historians, sociologists, and political scientists have all found new uses in the past six or seven decades for the *concept* of consensus. Consensus historians have developed what they regard as a healthy corrective for the tendency among their colleagues to emphasize conflict as an explanation for human history. Consensus sociologists have crafted theories of the shared normative commitments that they see undergirding modern societies and that explain such stability as they show. Consensus political scientists use the concept as the central element in descriptions of modern political cultures, the institutional arrangements they produce, and the decision processes they employ. Since the middle of the twentieth century, the concept of consensus has become integral to our arguments about how we should understand who we have been, who we are now, and who we might hope to become. How, then, does the concept of consensus inform and, indeed, undergird international regime formation and the process of legal restatement? And does this suggest a way forward in the development of global environmental rights?

International Regime Formation

Increasingly, "we live in a world of international regimes" (Young 1980, 331). Because these regimes vary greatly in terms of their "functional scope, areal purview and membership," the fundamental character of these regimes "remains elusive" (331–332). That this should be true in spite of the large and growing literature on the subject is somewhat disturbing. It suggests that many (perhaps even most) of those who have written on the subject have been mutually incomprehensible to one another in one way or another. But, in their defense, the subject of their study seems no more comprehensible. With environmental policy as the fundamental concern, a survey of the various arrangements for global environmental governance finds "overlap and duplication, fragmentation, redundancy, and multiple arenas at multiple levels" – in short, a complete absence of the order and rationality "that would come with the dominance of a single governance institution" or controlling legal order (Kellow 2012, 330). Moreover, the realm of international environmental law, which ultimately must sustain international environmental human rights, seems to be entirely without the ability to organize itself, let alone to chart a coherent (much less reliably progressive) course. Even as a nominal label, it seems to fail us across the board. Which form of the international are we referring to? "That of free trade or human rights? Security, science, or mass media? The international of the EU or Nokia; of Amnesty or Al-Qaida" (Koskenniemi 2009, 28)?

This framing of international regime formation is, indeed, discouraging. But before surrendering to the quiet desperation that any attempt to swallow globalization whole must entail, it is probably worthwhile to attempt some conceptual clarification – and simplification – that might offer useful analytical options. Regimes are informal arrangements, nothing more than "social institutions governing the actions of those interested in specifiable activities (or meaningful sets of activities)" and, as such, they are merely "recognized patterns of practice around which expectations converge" (Young 1980, 332). Of course, some aspects of regimes are highly formalized, such as treaties and international intergovernmental agencies, and some participants in regimes are formally created actors, such as scientific institutes and associations, multinational corporations, and NGOs, but regimes themselves are informal arrangements. Recognizing international regimes generally as social constructs allows us to understand them as a subset of those constructs that pertain to "activities that take place entirely outside the jurisdictional boundaries of sovereign states ... or cut across international jurisdictional boundaries ... or involve actions having a direct impact on two or more members of the international community" (333). From this perspective, international regimes appear as pragmatic arrangements designed to pursue shared interests (even if the interest is the maintenance of a competitive process) and constructed within a framework of empirical facts about what works (and does not work) in practice. Each of these components – shared interests and empirical facts – is worth exploring in more detail.

International regimes protect shared interests through rules. The best test for determining the existence of a rule in international law is what might be called the "authority-control test" (Arend 1999, 87). Put simply, there is an international rule (founded on the Trail Smelter case) that prohibits one state from causing environmental damage in another, but there is no international rule that imposes a duty on states to combat climate change. To demand more real-world impact of international rules is to hold them to a higher standard than we do domestic rules. After all, no one doubts the legal character of a highway speed limit simply because it is widely ignored and rarely if ever enforced. The reason for this is clear. Both kinds of rule actually succeed when they are followed tolerably well with little or no enforcement. But international rules differ in some important ways from other rules, and these differences must be accounted for because they are important for understanding shared interests and empirical facts as the primary components of international regimes.

To extend our comparison of international regimes and domestic traffic rules, consider again speeding motorists. By significantly exceeding the speed limit, they fail to advance the interests that they share with other motorists by rendering the safe operation of a vehicle on a public thoroughfare more difficult. That the letter of this law is almost never enforced shows unmistakably that the mere assertion of authority is not the point of the rule. The point is to facilitate a shared activity that has high social value. For that reason, meticulous enforcement is actually self-defeating because it would be a serious misallocation of resources and would likely engender resentment of the rule itself. But the rule is recognized as authoritative (as can be inferred from the motorist's participation in the entire regime of traffic regulation). It affects the behavior of those to whom it is addressed because there is a threshold beyond which the factual circumstances of each individual motorist's participation in the social system sustained by the rule will be altered by the imposition of costs associated with sufficiently serious forms of noncompliance. This element of "facticity" in the law (Habermas 1996), as well as its empirical foundation in the potentially grisly consequences of a traffic system's failure, constitute the empirical component of domestic traffic regimes.

In comparison with domestic traffic regimes, international regimes display many similarities, with a few important differences. Like domestic rule systems, international regimes are dependent for their success upon "the maintenance of convergent expectations among actors" and are social systems that are "created rather than discovered" (Young 1980, 355). Also like domestic rule structures, international regimes often rely upon the convergent expectations of its actors and the compliance incentives that they create (338–342), rather than upon strict enforcement mechanisms (which will often raise the cost of reaching agreement on the regime to intolerable levels). Domestic traffic regulation regimes rarely display the same extent of "overlap and duplication, fragmentation, redundancy and multiple arenas at multiple levels" or any of the other forms of policy irrationality that one finds in the absence of "a single governance institution" that exercises full jurisdiction over the entire regime (Kellow 2012, 340). In the case of international regimes, however, levels of integration that are typical of domestic regimes are often impossible and there are often significant benefits to what would ordinarily be regarded as organizational dysfunctions (Young 1980). Even with respect to substantive rule ambiguity, the international arena imposes its own demands. Many of the ambiguities that regime scholars complain of are traceable to underlying limitations in the consensus supporting the regime. This underlying heterogeneity often prevents the use of less ambiguous vocabulary and reminds us that "the almost exclusive attention to norms and norm entrepreneurship" in parts of the regime literature ignores how vital the role of shared interests can be in determining "regime emergence, evolution and design" (Hansen 2016, 211).

To offer but one example, corporate bankruptcy law remained stubbornly resistant to internationalization until the globalization of investment capital made the unlimited diversity of legal practice unsustainable. Even then, however, the emergence of a consensus approach to the issue was characterized by a high level of recursivity – in which a continual process of dialogue, interpretation, and change occurred between the transnational, the national law-on-the-books, and the law-in-action affecting corporate practice (Halliday and Carruthers 2009). Is it surprising, then, that international processes for addressing climate change have remained mostly silent on the subject of a substantive environmental right to a sustainable climate? In spite of the broad awareness and wide discussion of the environmental human rights implications of climate change, UN Framework Convention on Climate Change actors have been stubbornly resistant to engaging the issue and are likely to remain so – given how much more complex the problem is than corporate bankruptcy and the extent to which financial motives mitigate against (rather than for) a resolution.

The issue of recursivity focuses attention on another important topic – the manner in which international regimes come into existence. Due, at least in part, to the dominance of social scientists in developing the regime formation literature, that research tradition has been largely preoccupied with the dichotomy between institutional change and institutional reproduction as frameworks for interpreting the formalization of international politics. It is a peculiar characteristic of law, however, that rules and norms are continually tested in relation to real cases. This feature of the regime formation environment has recently shifted some scholarly attention away from discussion of the change/reproduction argument toward a more consequentialist and incrementalist approach. The result is a view of regime formation that allows for a more or less settled consensus that is, nevertheless, susceptible to periodic reassessment as a consequence of changes in power distribution or other elements of the international bargaining environment (Thelen 2009). This broader and more flexible approach also allows for a better understanding of the degree to which "tipping point" developments in the conditions of global markets that determine the interests of multinational firms and their host states can alter the dynamics of international negotiation by fundamentally altering states' calculations of their interests in any given negotiation (Vormedal 2010). It also provides a context for the observation that the behavior of states with respect to regime ratification can be highly idiosyncratic and can depend as much on relations with other states and their ratification decisions as with domestic considerations of political ideology or economic interest (Perrin and Bernauer 2010).

Thus, there is a tension between the aspiration to facticity in international regimes and the awareness that recursive and incremental regime development often produces positive results and is sometimes the only approach to regime development. To put the matter more bluntly, how much of the character of a normative fact are we willing to surrender for the sake of practicality and power politics? In order to better appreciate this conundrum, which is in the very nature of regimes as social constructions, it is useful to consider the processes by which normative material works its way from individual commitments to international agreements. Examination of the process of legal restatement makes this more concrete and accessible, and completes the framing of human rights narratives as regions of normative consensus.

Restatement: Stating the Obvious

In 1923, a group of prominent US judges, lawyers, and teachers established ALI, the American Law Institute (see Baber and Bartlett 2009, 128–128; 2015, 123–125). The intention was to address what these founders took to be the two chief defects in American law at that time – its uncertainty and its complexity. *Uncertainty* in the law they attributed to a lack of agreement among members of the profession on the fundamental principles of the common law, a lack of precision in the use of legal terminology, poorly constructed and often conflicting statutory provisions, the large and growing volume of reported cases, and a relentless flow of novel legal questions (largely as a consequence of social change and economic growth). *Complexity* in the law, on the other hand, was attributed largely to its lack of systematic development and to its variation across the various jurisdictions comprising America's federal system of government. Against this backdrop, ALI undertook the improvement of law and its administration by promoting the clarification and simplification of the law and its better adaptation to social needs.

Since that time, the ALI's major tools for accomplishing its objective have been codification and restatement. Of the two, *codification* is the process that is more familiar to the world's legal community – for the simple reason that law-making through legislation has long been understood to be a core element of the rule of law. As practiced by the ALI, however, codification is entirely preliminary to legislation. As an example, in partnership with the National Conference of Commissioners on Uniform State Law, ALI developed the Uniform Commercial Code (UCC) – a comprehensive system of rules covering most aspects of modern commercial law. Like other ALI-developed model codes, the UCC goes beyond describing the current state of the law to identify what its authors take to be modern best practices in the law. In deploying this technique, ALI has limited itself to areas of the law where substantive uniformity is a desirable end in itself or where there is a general view that doctrinal reform is much needed.

The second tool of the ALI – *restatement* – has been deployed far more widely than has codification. A restatement is essentially a reference tool that presents the result of a careful survey of the existing state of the common law in a particular field of practice. Its purpose is to tell judges and lawyers what the law is in its current form. Between 1922 and 1944, the ALI developed 'Restatements of the Law' in the areas of agency, conflict of laws, contracts, judgments, property, restitution, security, torts, and trusts. In 1952, work began on the 'Restatement Second', reflecting both new analysis based on ongoing developments and the addition of coverage in such areas as landlord–tenant law and foreign relations law. The 'Restatement Third' was inaugurated in 1987, adding coverage of unfair competition, the law governing lawyers, and employment law.

The singular characteristic of the restatements has been their descriptive character. Where significant differences exist between jurisdictions on important points of law, those differences are noted and the restatement report generally limits its editorializing to the characterization of one view as the majority position. But whether this restraint is appropriate and sufficient has become a point of contention over the years. One of the major complaints about the restatements is that they have become far too progressive in their orientation, going well beyond describing the law as it is and advocating law as it ought to be. Originally viewed as the grand doctrinal voice of the common law (Smith 2012), the restatement project fell under the influence of legal realism (so the criticism goes). The promise was alluring. If only the study and practice of law "took account of the world outside the courtroom, it could contribute to revolutionary social changes" (Tilley 2017, 1403). If we could simply free ourselves from the idea that legal doctrine is handed down as "abstract rules unconnected to realities of the parties" it governs, legal doctrine could be "reimagined as a sort of analytical conveyor belt that routes instrumental insights to institutions that can deploy them for the unique purposes of the law" (1403).

For some critics, this turn of events raises nothing more serious than the concern that some reporters of the restatements may color their analysis to reach their desired conclusions – a problem that could easily enough be alleviated with rigorous and systematic reviews (Baude, Chilton, and Malani 2017). Others find the 'pluralism' of the legal realists far more troubling – a challenge to their basic worldview. Characterized uncharitably, these are legal absolutists, who believe "that there is one right way to understand the world or the law" and can never accept the idea that there are "multiple co-existing ways of knowing what counts as good law" (Smith 2012, 917). More charitably, this reaction against legal pluralism may be simply an artefact of social evolution. Taking the United States as an example, in the founding period of the nation's legal order, the country was "home to a multiplicity of closed communities featuring personal ties and moral solidarity" that established local expectations for individual behavior and thus interpretations of the law. Social development led to the evolution of a second-tier community that was "more heterogeneous, migratory, and lacked moral solidarity." Legal doctrine at this second level increasingly viewed the legitimacy of law "as contingent on its capacity to realize extra-legal goals" such as economic efficiency (Tilley 2017, 1403). Many critics of the restatements suspect their reporters of harboring precisely this attitude, a kind of ad hoc pluralism that has nothing to do with the orderly administration of law (as they understand it).

Yet another prominent criticism of the restatement project is that it is not progressive enough. The variations on this theme are many, including (1) that the drafters are overwhelmingly elite and hence elitist; (2) that the restatements' original purpose was progressive, and that they have failed in this; (3) that they 'reify' essentially the law and legal profession rather than trying to incorporate 'real-world' empirical insights from other disciplines; (4) that they have insulated the law from more aggressive reform; (5) that they are based on the illusion that the common law is more rational than it actually is or can be; and (6) that they lag behind the 'real-world' concerns of practicing lawyers (Adams 2007). This collection of complaints is, of course, overlapping in some regards and contradictory in others. They suggest that the restatement project, despite lofty reformist intentions, has been coopted by the legal establishment to insulate itself from criticism – indeed, from change in any form. These criticisms are not easy to assess. How much 'progress' is too much or too little seems a hopelessly abstract conversation, as does the charge that sustained analysis of admittedly conceptual subject matter runs the risk of reification (whatever that might mean in this context). An excess of rationality and an indifference to practical concerns may seem to be reinforcing tendencies in some circumstances and conflicting with them in others – making an aggregate judgment nearly impossible and almost certainly unenlightening. So, as with international regime formation, legal restatement faces its own struggles to reconcile the aspiration to universality with the appeal of particularity.

Perhaps the most instructive example of the problem is the climate and human rights connection. The International Law Commission's work is an example of the core difficulty. It assumes, as much study of international law does, that the field is fundamentally transactional rather than normative. Bridging that gap at the bottleneck of our hourglass in Figure 1 is simply not the point of transactional law-making. Rather, the point is to pound ongoing negotiating processes into a shape that can be described in the abstract (without introducing new controversies). When it comes to climate rights jurisprudence, it is about finding strategies that make the most of what we have – that is, what good environmental outcomes can be produced with existing human rights provisions, given the special concerns of the tribunal involved. It is not about building a normative environmental human rights structure (from the ground up or in any other direction). Condemning international tribunals for not doing so is unfair and makes no sense. Blaming international bureaucrats for not being able to distill anything normatively intelligible from a transactional tangle is worse still. The normative content is missing (squeezed out at the bottleneck), so no genuine environmental human rights standards are advanced. When a process ceases to be normative and becomes wholly transactional, the human rights game has ended and the international relations game has begun – precisely because we have given up on the idea of normative consensus (in the face of the invocation of diversity as an insurmountable obstacle to human rights universality).

'Adjudicatory' research techniques can be used to see if there is (in fact) a substructure of normative consensus beneath all of the surface-layer diversity in human society (Baber and Bartlett 2009, 2015). If such a consensus exists anywhere it should be in the environmental arena – simply because nature constrains our options and (eventually) focuses our attention. Any such consensus should achieve its normatively richest state when our attention narrows down to issues of environmental human rights, which have a stronger moral thread than do transactional concerns.

This multilevel representation of global norm-building obviously does not answer all the questions that might reasonably be asked. The largest regions of uncertainty in Figure 1 unquestionably involve the voids that make up the top and bottom halves of our 'governance hourglass'. Who occupies those regions in the policy space? How do they interact with one another? Do they participate in the norm-building process on both sides of the elected official bottleneck? If so, does the role they play differ in those two different arenas? Perhaps most important, is there any way that this conception of global norm-building can be used by those whose objective is to nudge the governance process in the direction of outcomes that are more environmentally friendly and provide better protection for important human rights? These are not the only questions this Element leaves unanswered. But they identify the major concerns for what must follow in any collective effort of humanity to theorize, experiment, and analyze what will be necessary to establish the rights foundations of successful democratic earth system governance. Neither environmentalists nor human rights advocates should be surprised to learn that answers are unlikely to be either conceptually simple or universally applicable.

5 Conclusion

What are some of the key conceptual issues that would present themselves if the environmental challenges confronting humanity were reimagined as matters of human rights rather than merely as ecological/environmental goods (and bads)? This is a timely question to ask. As perhaps the most important indicator, environmental justice has become an increasingly vital part of the language of environmental activism, political debate, academic research, and policy-making around the world. Environmental justice narratives have traced their way across the globe and across scales of governance, taking up ecological issues of transnational concern, and examining research, activism, and policy development in widely diverse countries (Walker 2012). Environmental justice discourses have generally concentrated on environmental inequities related to race (Zimring 2016), indigeneity (Gilio-Whitaker 2019), and class (Robertson and Westerman 2015). But there is a growing awareness that various concrete manifestations are symptoms of a more general relationship between social inequity and environmental sustainability that eludes precise definition and evades conventional boundaries (Sze 2018). Indeed, under circumstances that are increasingly common, environmental injustice has come to be seen as part of a broader pattern of personal subjugation that amounts to violence against the individual (Pellow 2017).

It is against this increasingly important backdrop of environmental oppression that human environmental rights must be understood as part of a broader rights revolution (Section 2). Environmental human rights comprise 'policy spaces' in which there is some considerable congruence between the views of political leaders and those whom it is their duty to serve. This special category of rights lies at the intersection of a two-way instrumentality. Environmental rights both protect vital environmental interests *and* empower individuals to enjoy other fundamental rights that are not directly environmental in character.

Access to environmental information and decision-making and the rights to food and water are examples of such dual utility rights. Although commitments to provide access to information and decision-making are often the tribute paid to virtue by vice, and the obligation to provide the basic prerequisites of human survival is often treated as a custom to be honored more in the breach than the observance, it is still true that straightforward rejections of these rights are more and more difficult to find. An environmental right of even more general application would be environmental security – a rights discourse that, instead of asserting a substantive and *specific* environmental right, argues for a substantive and *general* one. A rights discourse such as this has the potential to help the foundational work in pursuit of rights that do not (yet) enjoy the support that comes with the immediacy and urgency of the need for food and water.

Two models, the declaratory and adjudicatory approaches to the development of human rights, work in opposite (although not necessarily inconsistent) directions along a continuum from the abstract theory to the concrete application, to which can be added the concept of reflexivity – having to do with the purpose(s) that narratives seek(s) to achieve (Section 3). Descriptive narratives aim only to mark out (call attention to) subject matter for those to whom it is addressed. Cognitive narratives also impose order on the policy arena that the narratives address, organizing its subject matter in ways that help addressees to better understand their situation in functional terms. Additionally, some rights narratives seek to add to the behavioral repertoire of its addressees – to increase their range of potential options for actually altering their situation. Taken together, these two dimensions of human rights discourses – level of abstraction and reflexivity – provide a useful framework for assessing across time and cultures whether rights narratives are fundamentally normative or analytical.

Armed with the normative-analytic typology that these dimensions describe, rights narratives, such as contemporary narratives of *environmental rights*, can be 'mapped' onto the conceptual space that the typology defines, gaining insight into the relative strengths (or advantages) and weakness (or disadvantages) of those narratives. A 'lightly populated' middle range of environmental rights narratives can be found lying between the *declaratory* approach of the Universal Declaration and the *adjudicatory* approach of the modern rights revolution (Section 4). A valid way to characterize this mid-range sort of narrative is that they need to be *deliberative* – that is to say, narratives of a discursive (rather than authoritative or imperative) character that rely on practical theorizing from the best available evidence and the testing of general maxims against the demands of particular cases. An in-depth analysis of instances of such deliberative narratives shows that they can usefully address many of the most challenging problems of securing environmental rights. In fact, they have the potential to establish a set of environmental rights principles – a new social consensus – grounded in an at least moderately progressive account of our history, a moderately pragmatic view of our present, and a moderately optimistic vision of our future (Wironen, Bartlett, and Erickson 2019).

The notion that there are (or might be) regions of environmental policy space in which deliberative agreement between mass and elite attitudes is sufficient to support the assertion of human environmental rights is based on the underlying assumption that *consensus* is not so rare a commodity as is customarily assumed. Why this assumption should strike so many as untenable is something of a mystery. Consider the following:

(1) Field studies by Elinor Ostrom and her colleagues (Ostrom 1990, 2005, Ostrom et al. 2002) suggest that successful institutions for the governance of natural resources can 'evolve' and be maintained at the community level without resort to coercive state power.

(2) Minimally coercive policy models such as environmental impact assessment and emissions trading schemes are found widely replicated across numerous jurisdictions and political systems (Stripple 2010).

(3) Since 1976, the right to live in a healthy environment has spread rapidly across the world, securing constitutional protection and being incorporated into national environmental laws in more than 140 countries, and gaining recognition in regional treaties ratified by at least 135 nations (Boyd 2012).

In the face of such data points, it seems implausible to argue that environmental consensus is rendered impossible by social, political, or historic forces that condemn us to unremitting conflict and the ecological losses that would impose.

A direct examination of consensus suggests that its history as a concept and the role it plays in three disciplines (history, sociology, and political science) can help us understand ourselves as a species. Consensus at the national level can find its way into law and repeat our agreement back to us (legal restatement). Transnational agreement on environmental problem-solving can support processes of consolidation and compromise that build shared institutional preferences into global policy norms (international regime formation). Norm formation that relates the local, the national, and the transnational rationalizes the ebb and flow from concrete problem-solving to abstract rule-making and back again. Functional relationships between adjudicatory and declaratory rights narratives, as well as the institutional forms particular to each, shows how they are linked through the deliberative intervention of formal government action.

There is a large and venerable literature that promotes the intrinsic *rights of nature* (whether nature as a whole, specific landscapes, types of species, or individual organisms). Arguments in this literature revolve around the moral consideration of nature, often using the shorthand 'rights' as a label – commonly (but dubiously) assuming that there will be direct and unproblematic political, sociological, and legal consequences of any such moral recognition. A second scholarly literature, which has mostly accumulated since 2000, identifies and charts the formal declarations of human environmental rights around the world, in statutory laws, court decisions, treaties, resolutions, and, particularly, in national constitutions. This literature is mostly descriptive and legalistic and is characterized by an unstated assumption that the widespread and repeated declaration of rights is the crucial step in the realization of such rights.

A third literature, on what has variably been called environmental, ecological, or sustainable democracy, offers a multiperspective analysis of the necessary normative and procedural foundations of any environmentally focused democracy. But this literature focuses overwhelmingly on democratic franchise, participation, process, and aggregation, with very little attention to two of the necessary prerequisites of enduring democratic practice, namely, establishment of the rule of law and a functional system of rights. For that reason, this third literature is unable (as it exists) to bridge the gap between concepts regarding the rights of nature and a declaratory model of human rights – neither of which have proven adequate to the task of establishing (as a fully functioning reality) the right to a healthy environment.

The path to a solution of this problem lies in three steps. First, understanding that the task of establishing a real, meaningful right to a healthy environment is an integral part of the broader human rights revolution. Doing so allows combining an adjudicatory model of rights with the declaratory model. This 'concretization' is essential if the two-way instrumentality of environmental human rights is to be widely recognized and the political advantages of that realization are to be enjoyed. Second, it is vitally important that we move beyond simplistic notions of how moral and ethical norms are converted into rights. An analytical model that details two processes of norm conversion (adjudicative and declarative) shows them moving in opposite but not opposing directions. Moreover, that model identifies a reflexive and recursive (*deliberative*) process of norm conversion that is hardly recognized because it lies nested between its two more newsworthy siblings. Third, the centrality of consensus is clear when one considers that the ultimate challenge for the establishment of real, effective human rights (environmental and otherwise) will always be regime formation and the full incorporation of rights in restatements. There is nothing in the history of democracy or diplomacy to suggest that either of these processes can succeed in the presence of significant and persistent dissent.

References

Adams, Kristen D. 2007. "Blaming the Mirror: The Restatements and the Common Law." *Indiana Law Review* 40:205–270.

Appiah, Kwame Anthony. 2005. *The Ethics of Identity*. Princeton, NJ: Princeton University Press.

Arend, Anthony Clark. 1999. *Legal Rules and International Society*. New York: Oxford University Press.

Arendt, Hannah. 1994 [1948]. *The Origins of Totalitarianism*. New York: Schoken.

Baber, Walter F., and Robert V. Bartlett. 2005. *Deliberative Environmental Politics: Democracy and Ecological Rationality*. Cambridge, MA: MIT Press.

Baber, Walter F., and Robert V. Bartlett. 2009. *Global Democracy and Sustainable Jurisprudence: Deliberative Environmental Law*. Cambridge, MA: MIT Press.

Baber, Walter F., and Robert V. Bartlett. 2015. *Consensus and Global Environmental Governance: Deliberative Democracy in Nature's Regime*. Cambridge, MA: The MIT Press.

Bardach, Eugene. 1978. *The Implementation Game: What Happens after a Bill Becomes a Law*. Cambridge, MA: MIT Press.

Barry, John. 2008. "Toward a Green Republicanism: Constitutionalism, Political Economy, and the Green State." *The Good Society* 17 (2):1–10.

Bartlett, Robert V. 1986. "Ecological Rationality: Reason and Environmental Policy." *Environmental Ethics* 8:221–239.

Baude, William, Adam Chilton, and Anup Malani. 2017. "Making Doctrinal Work More Rigorous: Lessons from Systematic Reviews." *University of Chicago Law Review* 84:37–58.

Bauhr, Monika, and Marcia Grimes. 2015. "Indignation or Resignation: The Implications of Transparency for Societal Accountability." *Governance: An International Journal of Policy, Administration, and Institutions* 27 (2):291–320.

Bell, Daniel. 1960. *The End of Ideology: On the Exhaustion of Political Ideas in the Fifties*. New York: Collier Books.

Bernard, Thomas. 1983. *The Consensus–Conflict Debate: Form and Content in Social Theories*. New York: Cambridge University Press.

Biermann, Frank. 2014. *Earth System Governance: World Politics in the Anthropocene*. Cambridge, MA: MIT Press.

Bodansky, Daniel. 2010. *The Art and Craft of International Environmental Law*. Cambridge, MA: Harvard University Press.

Boyd, David R. 2012. *The Environmental Rights Revolution: A Global Study of Constitutions, Human Rights, and the Environment*. Vancouver: University of British Columbia Press.

Boyd, David R. 2015. "Constitutions, Human Rights, and the Environment: National Approaches." In *Research Handbook on Human Rights and the Environment*, edited by Anna Grear and Louis J. Kotzé, 170–199. Cheltenham: Edward Elgar.

Burch, Sarah, Aarti Gupta, Cristina Y. A. Inoue, et al. 2019. "New Directions in Earth System Governance Research." *Earth System Governance* 1: 100006.

Chamberlain, Lisa. 2017. "Beyond Litigation: The Need for Creativity in Working to Realize Environmental Rights." *Law, Environment and Development Journal* 13 (1):1–12.

Claeys, Pricilla. 2015. *Human Rights and the Food Sovereignty Movement: Reclaiming Control*. New York: Routledge.

Cliteur, Paul. 2010. *The Secular Outlook: In Defense of Moral and Political Secularism*. Malden, MA: Wiley-Blackwell.

Collins, Randall. 1998. *The Sociology of Philosophies: A Global Theory of Intellectual Change*. Cambridge, MA: Harvard University Press.

Conca, Ken. 2015. *An Unfinished Foundation: The United Nations and Global Environmental Governance*. New York: Oxford University Press.

Dahl, Robert A. 1961. *Who Governs? Democracy and Power in an American City*. New Haven, CT: Yale University Press.

Dahl, Robert A. 1972. *Polyarchy: Participation and Opposition*. New Haven, CT: Yale University Press.

Dahl, Robert A. 1986. *A Preface to Economic Democracy*. Berkeley: University of California Press.

De Bary, William Theodore, and Weiming Tu, eds. 1998. *Confucianism and Human Rights*. New York: Columbia University Press.

Donnelly, Jack. 2013. *Universal Human Rights in Theory and Practice*. Ithaca, NY: Cornell University Press.

Dryzek, John S. 1987. *Rational Ecology: Environment and Political Ecology*. London: Basil Blackwell.

Dryzek, John S. 2010. *Foundations and Frontiers of Deliberative Governance*. New York: Oxford University Press.

Dryzek, John S. 2016. "Can There be a Human Right to an Essentially Contested Concept? The Case of Democracy." *Journal of Politics* 78 (2):357–367.

Duyck, Sébastien. 2015. "Promoting the Principles of the Aarhus Convention in International Forums: The Case of the UN Climate Change Regime." *Review of European Community and International Environmental Law* 22 (4):123–138.

Eckersley, Robyn. 2004. *The Green State: Rethinking Democracy and Sovereignty*. Cambridge: Cambridge University Press.

Eckersley, Robyn. 2017. "Geopolitan Democracy in the Anthropocene." *Political Studies* 65 (4):983–999.

Epp, Charles R. 1998. *The Rights Revolution: Lawyers, Activists, and Supreme Courts in Comparative Perspective*. Chicago: University of Chicago Press.

Epp, Charles R. 2009. *Making Rights Real: Activists, Bureaucrats, and the Creation of the Legalistic State*. Chicago: University of Chicago Press.

Fischer, Frank. 2003. *Reframing Public Policy: Discursive Politics and Deliberative Action*. New York: Oxford University Press.

Gellers, Joshua C. 2017. *The Global Emergence of Constitutional Environmental Rights*. New York: Routledge.

Gerber, Alan S., Gregory A. Huber, David Doherty, and Conor M. Dowling. 2011. "Citizens' Policy Confidence and Electoral Punishment: A Neglected Dimension of Electoral Accountability." *Journal of Politics* 73 (4):1206–1224.

Getliffe, Kate. 2002. "Proceduralisation and the Aarhus Convention." *Environmental Law Review* 4 (2):101–116.

Gewirth, Alan. 1983. *Human Rights: Essays on Justification and Applications*. Chicago: University of Chicago Press.

Gilio-Whitaker, Dina. 2019. *As Long as Grass Grows: The Indigenous Fight for Environmental Justice from Colonization to Standing Rock*. Boston: Beacon Press.

Glendon, Mary Ann. 1991. *Rights Talk: The Impoverishment of Political Discourse*. New York: Free Press.

Glendon, Mary Ann. 2002. *A World Made New: Eleanor Roosevelt and the Universal Declaration of Human Rights*. New York: Random House.

Goodin, Robert E., and John S. Dryzek. 2006. "Deliberative Impacts: The Macro-Political Uptake of Mini-Publics." *Politics & Society* 34 (2, June):219–244.

Gouveia, Cristina, Alexandra Foseca, António Câmara, and Francisco Ferreira. 2004. "Promoting the Use of Environmental Data Collected by Concerned Citizens Through Information and Communication Technologies." *Journal of Environmental Management* 71 (2):135–154.

Green, Jessica. 2014. *Rethinking Private Authority: Agents and Entrepreneurs in Global Environmental Governance*. Princeton, NJ: Princeton University Press.

Gregg, Benjamin. 2003. *Thick Moralities, Thin Politics: Social Integration Communities of Belief*. Durham, NC: Duke University Press.

Gregg, Benjamin. 2012. *Human Rights as Social Constructions*. Cambridge: Cambridge University Press.

Gregg, Benjamin. 2016. *The Human Rights State: Justice Within and Beyond Sovereign Borders*. Philadelphia: University of Pennsylvania Press.

Grob, Gerald, and George Billias, eds. 2000. *Interpretations of American History: Patterns and Perspectives*. New York: Free Press.

Gupta, Aarti, and Michael Mason. 2014. "A Transparency Turn in Global Environmental Governance." In *Transparency in Global Environmental Governance: Critical Perspectives*, edited by Aarti Gupta and Michael Mason, 3–38. Cambridge, MA: MIT Press.

Gupta, Joyeeta. 2016. "Toward Sharing our Ecospace." In *New Earth Politics: Essays from the Anthropocene*, edited by Simon Nicholson and Sikina Jinnah, 271–292. Cambridge, MA: MIT Press.

Habermas, Jürgen. 1979. *Communication and the Evolution of Society*. Boston: Beacon Press.

Habermas, Jürgen. 1996. *Between Facts and Norms: Contributions to a Discourse Theory of Law and Democracy*. Cambridge, MA: MIT Press.

Hajer, Maarten A. 1995. *The Politics of Environmental Discourse: Ecological Modernization and the Policy Process*. New York: Oxford University Press.

Halliday, Terence, and B. G. Carruthers. 2009. *Bankrupt: Global Lawmaking and Systemic Financial Crisis*. Stanford, CA: Stanford University Press.

Hansen, Sussane Therese. 2016. "Taking Ambiguity Seriously: Explaining the Indeterminacy of the European Union Conventional Arms Export Control Regime." *European Journal of International Relations* 22 (1):192–216.

Hartz, Louis. 1955. *The Liberal Tradition in America: An Interpretation of American Thought since the Revolution*. New York: Harcourt, Brace.

Hartz, Louis. 1964. *The Founding of New Societies: Studies in the History of the United States, Latin America, South Africa, Canada and Australia*. New York: Harcourt, Brace.

Hayward, Tim. 2000. "Constitutional Environmental Rights: A Case for Political Analysis." *Political Studies* 48 (3):558–572.

Hayward, Tim. 2016. "A Global Right of Water." *Midwest Studies in Philosophy* 40 (1):217–233.

Higham, John. 1959. "The Cult of the "American Consensus": Homogenizing Our History." Commentary 27 (February).

Hiskes, Richard. 2009. *The Human Right to a Green Future*. New York: Cambridge University Press.

Hofstadter, Richard. 1979. *The Progressive Historians: Turner, Beard, Parrington*. Chicago: University of Chicago Press.

Jonsen, Albert R., and Stephen Toulmin. 1990. *The Abuse of Casuistry: A History of Moral Reasoning*. Berkeley: University of California Press.

Keck, Margaret E., and Kathryn Sikkink. 2014. *Activists beyond Borders: Advocacy Networks in International Politics*. Ithaca, NY: Cornel University Press.

Kellow, Aynsley. 2012. "Multi-Level and Multi-Arena Governance: The Limits of Integration and the Possibilities of Forum Shopping." *International Environmental Agreements: Politics, Law and Economics* 12:327–342.

Kenniston, Kenneth. 1975. "Revolution or Counterrevolution?" In *Explorations in Psychohistory: The Wellfleet Papers*, edited by Robert Jay Lifton and Erik Olson, 293–294. New York: Simon and Schuster.

Kent, George. 2005. *Freedom from Want: The Human Right to Adequate Food*. Washington, DC: Georgetown University Press.

Klosko, George. 2000. *Democratic Procedures and Liberal Consensus*. New York: Oxford University Press.

Knox, John H. 2013. *Report of the Independent Expert on the Issue of Human Rights Obligations Relating to the Enjoyment of a Safe, Clean, Healthy and Sustainable Environment, Mapping Report*. New York: United Nations Human Rights Council.

Knox, John H. 2018. *Report of the Special Rapporteur on the Issue of Human Rights Obligations Relating to the Enjoyment of a Safe, Clean, Healthy and Sustainable Environment*. New York: United Nations, Human Rights Council.

Koskenniemi, Martti. 2009. "The Fate of Public International Law: Between Technique and Politics." *Modern Law Review* 70 (1):1–30.

Kotzé, Louis J. 2015. "Human Rights and the Environment through an Environmental Constitutional Lens." In *Research Handbook on Human Rights and the Environment*, edited by Anna Grear and Louis J. Kotzé, 145–169. Cheltenham: Edward Elgar.

Kysar, Douglas A. 2010. *Regulating from Nowhere: Environmental Law and the Search for Objectivity*. New Haven, CT: Yale University.

Leib, Linda. 2011. *Human Rights and the Environment: Philosophical, Theoretical, and Legal Perspectives*. Leiden Martinus Nijhoff.

Lijphart, Arend. 1976. *The Politics of Accommodation: Pluralism and Democracy in the Netherlands*. 2nd ed. Berkeley: University of California Press.

Lijphart, Arend. 1984. *Democracies: Patterns of Majoritarian and Consensus Government in Twenty-One Countries*. New Haven, CT: Yale University Press.

Lipset, Seymour Martin. 1975. "Social Structure and Social Change." In *Approaches to the Study of Social Structure*, edited by Peter M. Balu, 172–209. New York: Pree Press.

Lipset, Seymour Martin. 1977. "'The End of Ideology' and the Ideology of Intellectuals." In *Culture and Its Creators*, edited by Joseph Ben David and Terry Clark, 15–42. Chicago: University of Chicago Press.

Lipset, Seymour Martin. 1979. "Predicting the Future of the Post-Industrial Order: Can We Do It?" In *The Third Century: America as a Post-Industrial Society*, edited by Seymour Martin Lipset, 1–35. Stanford, CA: Hoover Institution Press.

McAdam, Jane. 2012. *Climate Change, Forced Migration, and International Law*. New York: Oxford University Press.

McGee, Rosemary. 2004. "Unpacking Policy: Actors, Knowledge and Spaces." In *Unpacking Policy: Actors, Knowledge and Spaces*, edited by Karen Brock, Rosemary McGee, and John Gaventa, 1–26. Cambridge, MA: MIT Press.

Merton, Robert K. 1957. *Social Theory and Social Structure*. Glencoe, IL: Free Press.

Meyer, John M. 2015. *Engaging the Everyday: Environmental Social Criticism and the Resonance Dilemma*. Cambridge, MA: MIT Press.

Morrow, Karen. 2015. "Sustainability, Environmental Citizenship Rights, and the Ongoing Challenge of Reshaping Supranational Environmental Governance." In *Research Handbook on Human Rights and the Environment*, edited by Anna Grear and Louis J. Kotzé, 200–218. Cheltenham: Edward Elgar.

O'Neill, Kate. 2016. "Institutional Politics and Reform." In *New Earth Politics: Essays from the Anthropocene*, edited by Simon Nicholson and Sikina Jinnah, 157–182. Cambridge, MA: MIT Press.

Ostrom, Elinor. 1990. *Governing the Commons: The Evolution of Institutions for Collective Action*. New York: Cambridge University Press.

Ostrom, Elinor. 2005. *Understanding Institutional Diversity*. Princeton, NJ: Princeton University Press.

Ostrom, Elinor, Thomas Dietz, Nives Dolsak, et al., eds. 2002. *The Drama of the Commons*. Washington, DC: National Academy Press.

Parsons, Talcott. 1951. *The Social System*. Glencoe, IL: Free Press.

Parsons, Talcott. 1961. "An Outline of the Social System." In *Theories of Society: Foundations of Modern Sociological Theory*, edited by

Talcott Parsons, Edward Shils, Kasper D. Naegele, and Jesse R. Pitts, 30–79. New York: Free Press.

Parsons, Talcott. 1969. *Politics and Social Structure*. New York: Free Press.

Parsons, Talcott. 1971. *The System of Modern Societies*. Englewood Cliffs, NJ: Prentice-Hall.

Pellow, David Naguib. 2017. *What is Critical Environmental Justice?* Cambridge: Polity.

Perrin, Sophie, and Thomas Bernauer. 2010. "Internartional Regime Formation Revisited: Explaining Ratification Behaviour with Respect to Long-Range Transboundary Air Pollution Agreements in Europe." *European Union Politics* 11 (3):405–426.

Perry, Mark. 2016. "Sustaining Food Production in the Anthropocene: Influences by Regulation of Crop Biotechnologie." In *Food Systems Governance: Challenges for Justice, Equality and Human Rights*, edited by Amanda Kennedy and Jonathan Liljeblad, 127–142. New York: Routledge.

Posner, Eric A. 2009. *The Perils of Global Legalism*. Chicago: University of Chicago Press.

Posner, Eric A. 2014. *The Twilight of Human Rights Law*. New York: Oxford University Press.

Rawls, John. 1971. *A Theory of Justice*. Cambridge, MA: Harvard University Press.

Rawls, John. 1993. *Political Liberalism*. New York: Columbia University Press.

Riol, Katherine S. E. Cresswell. 2016. *The Right to Food Guidelines, Democracy and Citizen Participation: Country Case Studies*. New York: Routledge.

Risse, Thomas. 2014. "No Demos? Identities and Public Spheres in the Euro Crisis." *Journal of Common Market Studies* 52 (6):1207–1215.

Risse, Thomas, Stephen C. Ropp, and Kathryn Sikkink, eds. 1999. *The Power of Human Rights: International Norms and Domestic Change*. New York: Cambridge University Press.

Robertson, Chistina, and Jennifer Westerman, eds. 2015. *Working on Earth: Class and Environmental Justice*. Reno: University of Nevada Press.

Rorty, Richard. 1989. *Contingency, Irony, and Solidarity*. New York: Cambridge University Press.

Salmon, Salmon M. A., and Siobhan McInerney-Lankford. 2004. *The Human Right to Water: Legal and Policy Dimensions*. New York: World Bank Publications.

Shils, Edward. 1961. "Epilogue." In *Theories of Society: Foundations of Moderns Sociological Theory*, edited by Talcott Parsons, Edward Shils, Kasper D. Naegele, and Jesse R. Pitts. Glencoe, IL: Free Press 1405–1450.

Sikkink, Kathryn. 1998. "International Norm Dynamics and Political Change." *International Organization* 52 (4):887–917.

Sikkink, Kathryn. 2017. *Evidence for Hope: Making Human Rights Work in the 21st Century*. Princeton, NJ: Princeton University Press.

Smith, Lionel. 2012. "Legal Epistemology in the Restatement (Third) of Restitution and Unjust Enrichment." *Boston University Law Review* 92 (3):899–917.

Staszak, Sarah. 2015. *No Day in Court: Access to Justice and the Politics of Judicial Retrenchment*. New York: Oxford University Press.

Sternsher, Bernard. 1975. *Consensus, Conflict, and American Historians*. Bloomington: Indiana University Press.

Stiglitz, Joseph E. 2017. *Globalization and Its Discontents Revisited: Anti-Globalization in the Era of Trump*. New York: W. W. Norton.

Stripple, Johannes. 2010. "Weberian Climate Policy: Administrative Rationality Organized as a Market." In *Environmental Politics and Deliberative Democracy: Examining the Promise of New Modes of Governance*, edited by Karin Backstrand, Jamil Kahn, Annica Kronsell, and Eva Lovbrand, 67–84. Cheltenham: Edward Elgar.

Sze, Julie, ed. 2018. *Sustainability: Approaches to Environmental Justice and Social Power*. New York: New York University Press.

Thelen, Kathleen. 2009. "Institutional Change in Advanced Political Economies." *British Journal of Industrial Relations* 47 (3):471–498.

Thielborger, Pierre. 2014. *The Right(s) to Water: The Multilevel Governance of a Unique Human Right*. Berlin: Springer-Verlag.

Tilley, Cristina. 2017. "Tort Law Inside Out." *Yale Law Journal* 126 (5): 1320–1406.

Turner, Stephen J. 2014. *A Global Environmental Right*. New York: Routledge.

UNEP. 2014. *UNEP Compendium on Human Rights and the Environment*, edited by United Nations Environment Programme and Center for International Environmental Law. Nairobi: United Nations Environment Programme.

Vormedal, Irja. 2010. "States and Markets in Global Environmental Governance: The Role of Tipping Points in Regime Formation." *European Journal of International Relations* 18 (2):251–275.

Walker, Gordon. 2012. *Environmental Justice: Concepts, Evidence and Politics*. New York: Routledge.

Walzer, Michael. 2007. *Thinking Politically: Essays in Political Theory*. New Haven, CT: Yale University Press.

Weatherall, Thomas. 2015. *Jus Cogens: International Law and Social Contract*. New York: Cambridge University Press.

Wernaart, Bart F. W. 2014. *The Enforceability of the Human Right to Adequate Food: A Comparative Study*. Wageningen: Wageningen Pers.

Westra, Laura. 2011. *Human Rights: The Commons and the Collective*. Vancouver: University of British Columbia Press.

Winkler, Inga T. 2012. *The Human Right to Water: Significance, Legal Status and Implications for Water Allocation*. Oxford: Hart.

Wironen, Michael B., Robert V. Bartlett, and Jon D. Erickson. 2019. "Deliberation and the Promise of a Deeply Democratic Sustainability Transition." *Sustainability* 11 (4): 1023.

Wolin, Sheldon. 2004. *Politics and Vision: Continuity and Innovation in Western Political Thought*. Princeton, NJ: Princeton University Press.

Wolin, Sheldon. 2008. *Democracy Incorporated: Managed Democracy and the Specter of Inverted Totalitarianis*. Princeton, NJ: Princeton University Press.

Wollstonecraft, Mary. 2008 [1790–1794]. *A Vindication of the Rights of Women and a Vindication of the Rights of Man*. New York: Oxford University Press.

Young, Oran R. 1980. "International Regimes: Problems of Concept Formation." *World Politics* 32 (3):331–356.

Zimring, Carl. 2016. *Clean and White: A History of Environmental Racism in the United States*. New York: New York University Press.

Acknowledgments

Versions of this Element were presented at annual conferences of the Earth System Governance Project. Among others we thank Robyn Eckersley, Jonathan Pickering, Hayley Stevenson, and four anonymous reviewers for critical comments about the work. An early version of much of Section 2 was presented at a workshop on ecological democracy in Sydney, Australia and published as an article in *Journal of Environmental Policy & Planning*. Baber thanks the US Commission for the International Exchange of Scholars, the Swedish Fulbright Commission, and the Raoul Wallenberg Institute for Human Rights and Humanitarian Law for the 2017/2018 Fulbright Lund Chair of Public International Law, during which time he drafted his contribution to this volume. He also thanks Wallenberg Institute colleagues Alejandro Fuentes and Radu Mares for their many helpful discussions. Bartlett thanks the US Commission for the International Exchange of Scholars, the Austrian–American Educational Commission (FulbrightAustria), and the Diplomatic Academy of Vienna for providing the support and conducive circumstances that made his work on this project possible during an appointment as 2019 Fulbright-Diplomatic Academy Visiting Professor of International Studies.

About the authors

Walter F. Baber a Professor in the Environmental Sciences and Policy Program and the Graduate Center for Public Policy and Administration at California State University, Long Beach. He is also an Affiliated Professor at the Raoul Wallenberg Institute of Human Rights and Humanitarian Law in Lund, Sweden. He has published many research articles and five previous books, including four co-authored with Robert V. Bartlett – most recently: *Environmental Human Rights in Earth System Governance: Democracy Beyond Democracy* (Cambridge University Press, 2020) and *Consensus and Global Environmental Governance: Deliberative Democracy in Nature's Regime* (MIT Press, 2015). He has been a Lead Faculty of the international Earth System Governance research alliance since 2012.

Robert V. Bartlett is the Gund Professor of the Liberal Arts in the Political Science Department and the Environmental Program at the University of Vermont, where he is also a Fellow in the Gund Institute of Environment. He has published many research articles and eleven books. He has been a Lead Faculty of the international Earth System Governance research alliance since 2012.

Elements of Earth System Governance

Frank Biermann
Utrecht University

Frank Biermann is Research Professor of Global Sustainability Governance with the Copernicus Institute of Sustainable Development, Utrecht University, the Netherlands. He is the founding Chair of the Earth System Governance Project, a global transdisciplinary research network launched in 2009; and Editor-in-Chief of the new peer-reviewed journal *Earth System Governance* (Elsevier). In April 2018, he won a European Research Council Advanced Grant for a research program on the steering effects of the Sustainable Development Goals.

Aarti Gupta
Wageningen University

Aarti Gupta is Associate Professor of Global Environmental Governance at the Environmental Policy Group of Wageningen University, the Netherlands. She has been a Lead Faculty in the Earth System Governance Project since 2014 and served as one of five Coordinating Lead Authors of the recently issued New Directions ESG Science and Implementation Plan. As of November 2018, she is a member of the ESG Project's Scientific Steering Committee. She is also Associate Editor of the journal *Global Environmental Politics*.

About the series

Linked with the Earth System Governance Project, this exciting new series will provide concise but authoritative studies of the governance of complex socio-ecological systems, written by world-leading scholars. Highly interdisciplinary in scope, the series will address governance processes and institutions at all levels of decision-making, from local to global, within a planetary perspective that seeks to align current institutions and governance systems with the fundamental 21st Century challenges of global environmental change and earth system transformations.

Elements in this series will present cutting edge scientific research, while also seeking to contribute innovative transformative ideas towards better governance. A key aim of the series is to present policy-relevant research that is of interest to both academics and policy-makers working on earth system governance.

More information about the Earth System Governance project can be found at: http://www.earthsystemgovernance.org

Cambridge Elements ≡

Elements of Earth System Governance

Elements in the series

Printed in the United States
By Bookmasters